LIVING WITH
CHRONIC PAIN
ONE DAY AT A TIME

Illustrations by
Timothy Schutz
Cover Artwork by
Maggie Rose

Freedom Enterprises

First printing January, 1994.

ISBN: 0-9637353-0-6
Printed in the United States of America

Freedom Enterprises in Chronic Pain
P.O. Box 40220
St. Paul, MN 55104

LIVING WITH CHRONIC PAIN ONE DAY AT A TIME

This book is dedicated in the memory of

Mike

ACKNOWLEDGMENTS

The following people have given their individual gifts to make this book possible:

Mom
Lynn
Maggie
Grandma Jean
Ted
Micky
Steve and Pam
Mike
Cindy
Dave
Carol
Molly
Rita

Introduction

I awoke one winters morning to the call of my pain, as I did the day before and the day before that. But this was to be remembered as a special day. With no warning my thoughts and emotions erupted. My journey towards the unknown was underway. Several months later, *"Living With Chronic Pain One Day At a Time"* became a reality. My hope is when you read these meditations, you will gain insight towards coping with your pain and discover the many personal changes we are asked to make in order to fulfill our emotional, physical, and spiritual needs.

I want to personally acknowledge my Higher Power, my friends, and the rest of my support system for guiding me through this process. But most of all, to those who picked me up when I had fallen and for reassuring me that if I believe in a purpose, it is worth the endeavor. For those who strive daily to manage their pain, for those who have come before us and those who are no longer with us, I am grateful to you all. We are all one, the ones who have chronic pain.

the author

JANUARY

As the New Year begins, we may feel the urge to look back and focus on what we fell short of accomplishing, rather than looking at what we have accomplished. Some of us may feel a sense of failure for not completing each and every task we set out to complete. Some of us may feel let down because what we thought was supposed to happen during the past year failed to materialize. We must be gentle with ourselves, for this is your new beginning.

Our past can be our wisdom and our teacher for today and in the year to come. We no longer need to look back with a sense of failure, but rather with a sense of pride and gratitude. We have learned the meaning of perseverance and we are the ones who have dared to move forward.

The New Year ahead promises opportunities for growth and new beginnings. Our task is to be open and willing to accept them as they cross our path. Am I open to new beginnings?

Higher Power, please help me learn from my past successes rather than dwell on the failures. Please help me be open to new beginnings that cross my path today and for the year ahead.

Higher Power, please help me cope with my pain today!

Looking back at our first days, weeks, and months with pain, can we see we have come a long way? Can we see we have come from a state of hopelessness to one of hope? From a place where dreams were nonexistent to a place where dreams are plentiful and real? Can we see we have come from a place where self respect and love for ourselves had ceased to exist to a place where we have grown to accept and love ourselves just as we are? Can we see we have come a long way?

Today is a day to look back to our beginning. A day to acknowledge the work we have done and to remember there is work that lies ahead. It is a day that each of us can stand proud and be grateful. For we truly have come a long way. Do I know I have come a long way?

High Power, please help me see that I have come a long way and that I couldn't have done it alone.

Higher Power, please help me cope with my pain today!

I have known you for some time and you have never left my side. You have been faithful and at times unfaithful. You have tested me many times, yet we are still together. I have fought you like no others, yet I have accepted you. Why, I am not sure. You have embarrassed me more than once and you have caused me more grief than any others. You have taken away my dreams many times, yet I continue to take you back. I know you are my pain and you will be with me for life, but somehow it doesn't seem fair. There are times when you have complete control over me and all my pleading has made little difference. I don't know why we have been introduced or what we are to learn and accomplish together. But for today, this is my admission to you. Have I grown to accept my pain?

Higher Power, please help me be honest with myself about my pain today.

Higher Power, please help me cope with my pain today!

Our graduation day does not consist of celebrating a totally pain free existence. But rather a day that we have come to accept our condition and it's limitations and it's many new possibilities. A day that we are no longer prisoners of our pain. A day that we have come to realize we have been given a second chance at life. A day that we begin to feel grateful for what we have rather than feeling bitter, spiteful, and angry for what we feel we should have.

Our graduation day is about what we have learned about ourselves and our pain. It is a day that we have worked towards for quite some time. It is a day that we can stand tall and be proud of the work we have done. For this is our graduation day. Am I waiting to celebrate a pain free existence or am I working towards learning about myself and my pain?

Higher Power, please give me the courage to continue to learn more about myself and my pain.

Higher Power, please help me cope with my pain today!

Looking beyond our pain is sure to be one of the most difficult tools to put into practice. Most of us have been focusing on our pain for some time. To begin focusing on other objects or other areas of our lives may seem impossible to us. At least in the beginning. We must remember, this is possible to learn, but it will take all the energy, patience, and willingness we have to begin looking beyond our pain.

Some of us may be saying, "You've got to be kidding." We're not. If we continue to focus on our pain and it's effects, we will continue to feel sorry for ourselves and remain prisoners of our pain. Today, we must begin looking beyond our pain and begin living our lives. Do I continue to focus on my pain today?

Higher Power, please teach me to look beyond my pain today.

Higher Power, please help me cope with my pain today!

Is there a cure for chronic pain? Most likely not. We have a chronic condition that will most likely be our partner for life. Many have tried to reverse the damage we have suffered but had little success. We have been told there is nothing that can be done. You'll just have to live with your injury and your pain. For many, this was unacceptable. We thought someone somewhere has to be able to do something.

This is true. Someone needs to do something. That someone is us. There may not be a cure for our condition, but there is a solution. We can learn to manage our pain and learn to live with it the best we can. Today we can live in the solution or we can continue to live in the problem. Have I accepted my condition for what it is?

Higher Power, please help me accept that my pain is chronic in nature. Help me realize there is a solution and that I can live within this solution or I can live within the problem.

Higher Power, please help me cope with my pain today!

Fear has struck each and every one of us with chronic pain. It has touched all areas of our lives. We feared our pain, our past, our present and future. We feared our family, our friends, our economic situations, and some of us were afraid of ourselves.

Our fear is natural. However, it becomes unhealthy when we let it run our lives and make all our decisions. Coming to terms with our fear will require us to look beyond the fear itself. Usually there is a secondary reason for our fear. When we discover what that is and face it, we no longer have to let our fear control our lives. We can make our own choices based on our thoughts, not our fear. Am I coming to terms with my fears today?

Higher Power, please give me the courage to come to terms with my fears and find the freedom to make my own choices.

Higher Power, please help me cope with my pain today!

I have come to accept that my pain will not fade or go away with time. I was told it would at one time, but it hasn't. I spent countless hours waiting and watching but nothing happened. It seemed like a life time that I waited and for what? I waited for my friends, but some never returned. I thought I waited long enough. Maybe not. I waited for all my dreams to come true but none of them materialized. Maybe I didn't wait long enough. I waited for what seems an eternity for my life to change in some small way but it remains the same. I don't understand. I thought time was to take care of all. I guess I'll have to wait for more time. Do I continue to wait or have I taken responsibility for my life?

Higher Power, please help me realize time will heal some wounds but not all situations.

Higher Power, please help me cope with my pain today!

When our pain had control of us our behavior was nothing short of self-centered and out-of-control. Now it is time to assess the damage and make peace. We need to ask ourselves where we went wrong in our actions. Who happened to be in our line of fire during the times we had blown up and who did we purposely set out to injure? By honestly asking ourselves these questions we can assess the damage we caused, make peace, and move on.

We might like to say, "Remember me? I am the one who is in pain here. I don't owe anyone anything." We may be in pain, that is true, but that doesn't give us a free pass to say and do as we please. If someone else treated us the way we may have treated others, chances are we would want them to acknowledge their wrongs to us. What is right for others is also right for us.

Have I assessed the damage I caused to myself and others?

Higher Power, please help me to look at the damage I have caused others. Please take away any defects that stand in my way of making amends to myself and others.

Higher Power, please help me cope with my pain today!

11

Our first step in recovery is to get our pain under control as best we can. The second step is changing parts of our personality. We must change ourselves to meet the conditions our new life dictates. We can no longer have an all or nothing attitude. Balance must become our common ground. We can no longer afford to leap without thinking of the consequences to our bodies. Seeking alternative ways to work and play must become second nature to us. Remember, our health depends on it.

Changing our personalities completely won't happen overnight. This is a process that will take patience and prayer if we are to succeed. Chances are, most of us will take steps backwards at first but in time our personalities can change. Do I need to change my way of thinking and acting?

Higher Power, please give me the courage and patience to change and adapt to my new way of living.

Higher Power, please help me cope with my pain today!

Some of us with chronic pain get stuck in the revolving door of hospital visits, doctors offices, and other institutions. We are determined not to give up until someone somewhere takes away our pain.

Chances are, if our pain is chronic it's for life and no one can take it away. There are no quick fixes in any one of the revolving doors. Just unfulfilled hopes and disappointment.

Recognizing and accepting there are no quick fixes and no one can take our pain away, will be one of the most difficult declarations we will face. But we also know this is our first step towards a new life. The life of acceptance and peace. Am I still using the revolving door for answers?

Higher Power, please help me accept that the answers I am searching for are within me. Help me realize that I have the ability to manage my pain today.

Higher Power, please help me cope with my pain today!

Most of us have learned that a moan here, a groan there, and other verbal outbursts will capture the attention of others. They tend to feel sorry for us and in turn, they want to help us or take care of us. This only feeds the cycle those of us with chronic pain must avoid.

We want to manage our pain, not focus on it or use it to gain the attention of others. When we do this, we are exhibiting pain behavior. We have fallen into a cycle that is sure to slow our progress and in some cases, push us further backwards.

The behaviors that we have learned can certainly be unlearned. But chances are, this won't happen immediately. If we are to change our pain behavior, it will take willingness, patience, and persistence on our behalf. For today, we can learn how to avoid our pain behavior. Have I broken the cycle of practicing pain behavior?

Higher Power, please help me avoid using pain behaviors today.

Higher Power, please help me cope with my pain today!

Some of us had a relationship with our Higher Power from the beginning. We have trusted, had faith and we have come to depend on our Higher Power. But others are not as fortunate. They stand alone and confused. They had turned away in anger when their pain was not removed and their lives returned to normal. Hate, bitterness, and blame had replaced the trust and faith they once had. Contacting their Higher Power was done only to tell him or her that they had let us down and to ask, "How could you have let this happen to me?"

Our relationship with our Higher Power today does not need to be based on hatred and blame. Rather on one of trust, love and acceptance. As our honesty and acceptance progresses, many of us will come to see that our Higher Power is not at fault for our situations, but rather our Higher Power is here to help and comfort us. Have I contacted my Higher Power today or have I turned away in anger and bitterness?

Higher Power, please be here for me today.

Higher Power, please help me cope with my pain today!

I am sorry for whatever I have done to you. It isn't that I don't love you, I'm just stubborn. I know nothing else. For if I did I would surely change. I know we will be friends for life and whatever you tell me or however you treat me, I won't go away. I am your pain. For whatever reason, we have become acquainted. Maybe we can help each other.

I know you don't like pain and I don't like hurting you. Maybe together we can learn to live with each other. But you should know that I'm capable of hurting you even when I don't want to. It's just that I'm unpredictable at times. But remember it could be worse. You could have the kind of pain that hates you. Do I believe my pain doesn't have to be my enemy?

Higher Power, please help me accept that my pain has become a part of me and that it doesn't have to be my constant enemy.

Higher Power, please help me cope with my pain today!

16

Those of us with chronic pain are at high risk for developing depression. The depression can be either long-term or short-term, mild or severe. However, depression doesn't necessarily need to warrant our departure from managing our pain or from life itself.

We don't have to fight with our depression and we don't have to run from it either. We simply accept our depression and do our best to overcome it. If our depression becomes unmanageable, we must be willing to seek the support that is needed. Our pride and fears must be cast aside or our depression could become our departure. Do I have a close eye on my depression today?

Higher Power, help me accept my depression for today. Please grant me the courage and strength to live my life to the fullest today.

Higher Power, please help me cope with my pain today!

17

I was a young man filled with hope and dreams. It seemed as if I had the world in the palm of my hand. With a snap of my fingers, my life changed. I had lost all hope and some had lost hope in me. My pain was out of control and my emotions soon followed. I was on my way to a place unknown, never to return.

I had tried in my own way to reach out to others, but failed. Looking back, maybe I could have tried a different approach, who knows. I chose my own path. I did what I thought I needed to do at the time.

Today, I know that different people and different systems have forgotten about me and why I chose the path I did, but I haven't forgotten and I never will. What path am I thinking about taking today?

Higher Power, please help me choose the path you have set for me. Please help me reach out to others and ask for help.

Higher Power, please help me cope with my pain today!

When sex and chronic pain become the topic, embarrassment and insecurities are usually the results. Some of us believe we no longer measure up to that beautiful sexy person we once were. We no longer felt desirable or capable. We began comparing ourselves to others hoping we would find someone that resembled ourselves. We concluded that our pain had made us less than normal and our sexuality would be altered forever.

Be patient. Rediscovering how we feel about our sexuality and rebuilding our self-esteem will be a process. With prayer and work on our behalf, we can regain our positive feelings about our sexuality and our self-esteem. We will no longer need to compare ourselves to others. We can learn to love and accept ourselves just as we are. Do I feel positive about my sexuality and self-esteem today?

Higher Power, please help me accept myself for who I am today.

Higher Power, please help me cope with my pain today!

Many of us have come to hate our pain like nothing we have ever hated before. We have gone to great lengths to protect and preserve the hate we have and why shouldn't we? Our pain has cost us our jobs, our families and friends, and in some cases, ourselves. Naturally we're going to hate our pain. But we can only hate so long and blame so many until our time comes when we must say to ourselves, "I surrender. I know hating you will not make you go away, but I know no other way, but to hate you". Do I hate my pain today?

Higher Power, please show me another way other than hate. Help me accept the consequences of my pain today.

Higher Power, please help me cope with my pain today!

Those of us who are moms or dads and have chronic pain may not have been the perfect parent at one time or another. The missed ball games and dance recitals are in the past and they cannot be recovered. All our wishing and hoping will not bring back what we have missed, nor will it ease our pain.

We can, however, attempt to explain to our children how our pain had altered our behavior and help them understand that life with us may be somewhat different from now on. We should tell them we will try our best, but they must try and remember that we are not perfect. Our children may not understand this at the time, but it is important that we, as parents, try to help them accept our imperfections just as we accept theirs. Have I accepted I am not the perfect parent?

Higher Power, please help me accept that my past actions have been less than perfect. Help me come to realize that in spite of my pain, I can be a loving and caring parent.

Higher Power, please help me cope with my pain today!

21

At one time or another we all have a fantasy about our pain disappearing and our lives returning to the way they were before our injury. This is quite healthy and quite normal. But when we continually live in this type of fantasy and refuse to accept the reality of our situations, we are clearly on a course of self-destruction.

Our denial and fantasies will assure us a life of broken dreams, unfulfilled expectations, and a life consumed with anger and blame. Some of us may even reach a point where reality and fantasy become indistinguishable. For those of us with chronic pain, our fantasies could become the end of our realities if we are not careful. Do I live in my fantasies or have I accepted my situation for what it is today?

Higher Power, please help me make the transition from my fantasies to reality.

Higher Power, please help me cope with my pain today!

Learning to manage our pain will not be easy. Nor will our recovery process. There will be many things asked of us that we will question and fight the importance of until the end. We will experience physical pain as well as emotional pain. We will fall to our knees several times only to be presented with the opportunity to rise to our feet again. We will truly come to know the meaning of no pain-no gain.

Many of us may be thinking, you've got to be kidding. We're not. Whatever we put into learning how to managing our pain and our recovery, is what we will get out of it. We truly understand the magnitude of what is being asked and the type of commitment our recovery requires, but we are also fully aware of the gains to be made. Have I made a true commitment to learning how to manage my pain and to my recovery?

Higher Power, please help me realize there are no free rides when it comes to managing my pain and my recovery.

Higher Power, please help me cope with my pain today!

The facts are simple but harsh. There is no cure for chronic pain. It's ours to live with each day and each night. It can and has proven to be deadly. Many have taken their own life because of the pain and emotional turmoil it brings. It has aided in destroying dreams and families and it has left some dependent on alcohol and drugs.

On the other hand, many have sought out to manage their pain and have been successful. They lead content, productive and serene lives. Many have found new and exciting interests. While others have discovered they have been freed from the pain and despair they once knew so well. Their pain had no longer controlled their every waking moment. They had found peace. Do I know the facts about chronic pain?

Higher Power, please help me gently open my eyes to the facts about chronic pain.

Higher Power, please help me cope with my pain today!

For most of us our lives at one time have been turned upside down. Our daily routines have stopped. Our social calendars have been open for quite some time. We had dropped those activities that made our days complete. The stability we once had has faded away to be replaced by uncertainty.

As we begin to manage our pain we also begin to rebuild the stability we so desire. But this can not come before we have learned to manage our pain. When our pain is controlling our every thought and action, stability is sure to be unreachable. Remember, regaining stability in our lives can only be accomplished one day at a time and one piece at a time. Do I believe stability will be restored in my life?

Higher Power, please restore wholeness and stability in my life today.

Higher Power, please help me cope with my pain today!

Sometimes we find ourselves obsessed with our pain. We try to figure out the whys and wherefores of it. The definition of our pain usually gets blown out of proportion due to fear and confusion. Simply put, P.A.I.N. is predictable, absolute, immediate and negotiable.

We know when we do certain things our pain increases, making it very predictable. We know that if our pain is of a chronic nature, it is absolute. It will probably stay with us forever. We know our pain is immediate. It doesn't wait for a convenient time to strike us. Finally, and most importantly, we know our pain is negotiable or manageable. Even with it's predictability, it's absoluteness, and its immediacy we are able to negotiate with our pain and go on with our lives. What is my definition of pain today?

Higher Power, please help me understand my definition of pain and help me keep my pain in its simplest form today.

Higher Power, please help me cope with my pain today!

26

Many of us will begin our spiritual journeys at different times and at different places, but the final goal can be the same for us all. That goal is to believe in a Power greater than ourselves. One who loves us, cares for us, and accepts us as we are. A power greater than ourselves that will guide us and teach us and grant us what we need and at times, what we want. A Power that will help us cope with our pain each day and one who will never leave our side, even when we demand it.

If we have not yet begun our spiritual journey, there is still time. Our Higher Power is patiently waiting for us. All that is required from us is the willingness to begin. Have I begun my spiritual journey?

Higher Power, please show me how and where I can begin my spiritual journey today.

Higher Power, please help me cope with my pain today!

I was a strong lad. I could do anything that was asked of me. I felt healthy and secure. But one winter day that had all changed. I was overcome by pain. I was no longer a strong lad and I could do nothing you had asked of me. My physical pain soon turned into emotional pain. I was lost and alone. I was frightened of the future and willing to do anything to escape the present. What was I to do?

As time passed, I once again became a strong lad, not so much physically as emotionally. My pain remains, but I cope with it the best I know how. My past has granted me wisdom and a desire to move forward. I no longer yearn for that person I once was but rather strive for that person I am capable of being. Am I the same person as I once was or am I striving towards being that person I am capable of being?

Higher Power, please help me gain wisdom from my past. Grant me strength and faith to move forward to becoming the person I am capable of being.

Higher Power, please help me cope with my pain today!

28

In time of personal growth many of us assume we need to see or hear what is taking place within us. If we cannot, we assume change is no longer taking place.

The miracle of silence is that change takes place without immediate notice. As we learn our day to day lessons, we are changing and growing from within. Sometimes we notice this and other times it is revealed to us through the miracle of silence.

When we became inpatient for change today, we must be patient and have faith. Miracles are taking place all around us. Sometimes quickly, sometimes slowly, but they do materialize if we let them. Do I believe in the miracle of silence?

Higher Power, please help me have faith and trust in your miracles of silence today.

Higher Power, please help me cope with my pain today!

Many of us can clearly remember the first time we experienced our pain. We can remember the feelings of being powerless. We can remember wanting our pain to go away but everything we had tried failed. We were powerless.

But the powerlessness did not stop with just our pain. It had filtered into our lives as well. We had become powerless over the doctors, the insurance people, our families, our friends, and ultimately the direction our lives were heading.

If today we truly do not remember what our powerlessness was like, we may be on our way back to experience more. Do I truly remember the powerlessness in my life?

Higher Power, please help me accept that my powerlessness is part of my past, my present and my future. Please help me realize how far I have come since my beginning and help me learn to use the control you have given me wisely.

Higher Power, please help me cope with my pain today!

When our pain controls our every thought and action, we become changed people. We have become prisoners of our pain. We begin feeling alone and that no one could possibly understand what we're going through. For many, hopelessness and depression followed. We had arrived deep, deep under our pain.

Our physical pain is but one symptom of our injuries. Underneath, lies our feelings and emotions. For many of us, they became prisoners of our pain just as we had. From time to time all that was let out was anger and self-pity. We had lost those feelings of love and happiness we once knew so well.

As we begin to break free from our pain, we will begin to discover that our feelings and emotions had never left us. They were buried deep, deep under our pain. Have I begun searching for my feelings and emotions that lie beneath my pain?

Higher Power, please reveal those feelings and emotions that lie beneath my pain.

Higher Power, please help me cope with my pain today!

I will never forget you. You have caused irreversible damage. You have taken away what was once a perfect life piece by piece. You have shadowed all the love and kindness I had with blame and bitterness. You've taken my hope and turned it into hopelessness. You have made my every move difficult at best. You have transformed my soul from one of deepness to one consumed with depression. You have made me and kept me prisoner of all that I never wanted or thought I would be. How will I ever forget you? You don't. You accept me. Have I grown to accept my pain?

Higher Power, please help me learn to accept my pain and all it has taken from me. Help me realize that in spite of my pain and what I may have lost, recovery for me is possible.

Higher Power, please help me cope with my pain today!

When we begin working with others who have chronic pain, some of us will see immediate results with the people we have worked with. We may tend to think we have just worked a miracle and we have been appointed God. This is hardly true. We have just given of ourselves as our Higher Power has instructed us to. We have shared our experiences, strengths, and hopes with them. No more.

We can be proud of the work we have done, but we cannot afford to begin taking credit for others' success. If we take credit for others' successes, then we must also take credit for others whom we assumed failed. To do this is playing God and not working with others. Do I work with others today?

Higher Power, please help me share my experiences, strengths, and hopes when working with others today. Help me accept that the results are of your will and not mine.

Higher Power, please help me cope with my pain today!

FEBRUARY

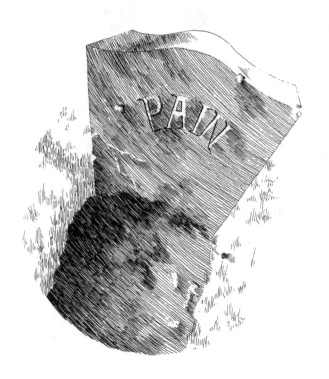

We can be going about our lives for days, months, and even years when suddenly, depression calls. All our plans become altered. Our bed becomes our domain. Our attitude and outlook on life change from one of hope to helpless. Our pain once again takes control as we are unable to muster up the energy to manage it. We have arrived at a place we once visited but were eager to leave. We asked ourselves how we could have returned to a place we so desperately avoided? Our answer, our depression called. Do I know what to do when my depression calls?

Higher Power, please help me ask for guidance and strength to seek support whenever my depression calls.

Higher Power, please help me cope with my pain today!

37

For many, the war within is with our acceptance of our injury and our pain. Some want so badly to believe their pain will one day disappear and that they will wake up from this painful nightmare and all will be the way it used to be. But night after night we are awakened only to be reminded it is not a dream.

There isn't anything anyone can do or any magical wand that will bring us instant acceptance of our condition. This is a process we must endure. But for others, it has become the war within. The war to end all wars. Coming to accept our injury and the pain we have will be one of the greatest challenges we may face. But we must keep our faith. There have been many who have won their war within and have learned to accept their condition. Have I learned to accept my injury and the pain I have today?

Higher Power, grant me the courage to accept my injury and my pain today.

Higher Power, please help me cope with my pain today!

The possibility for peace lies within all of us. We no longer have to live in constant fear and turmoil. Our path to peace will be through our Higher Power. When we begin to turn our will and our lives over to the care of our Higher Power, seek patience and have faith that we will be guided, we can discover the possibilities of peace.

But when we cast aside our Higher Power and take complete control of our lives, we may discover our possibilities for peace have diminished. Today the possibilities for inner peace are real. We can work towards peace in our lives or we can have turmoil, the choice is ours. Do I believe in the possibilities for peace in my life?

Higher Power, please grant me peace today. Help me do your will today and not mine.

Higher Power, please help me cope with my pain today!

Many of us say to ourselves, "I know I can do better if only I tried harder." This could be true. But all we're asked to do is the best we can.

We must realize that each day with chronic pain, doing the best we can changes. Yesterday we may have been able to work a full day and go out for the evening. Today the best we would do was go to work and survive the day. Tomorrow we may be able to do it all.

For today we must put forth our best effort and do the best we can. We need not compare ourselves with others performance or status. We have come a long way by doing the best we can one day at a time. Am I content with doing the best I can today or do I always want to do more?

Higher Power, please help me accept that I can only do my best today.

Higher Power, please help me cope with my pain today!

When we start our new life we are full of enthusiasm and excitement. We can't wait to make up for lost time. Watch out, we may be setting ourselves up. Moving too fast and trying to accomplish everything in one day can set us right back at the beginning. We can start falling short of all the things we set out to do. We end up telling ourselves, "I knew I couldn't do this. I knew I would never be able to manage my pain. My life will never get better."

If our attitude is one of impatience today, we are clearly in danger of setting ourselves up. We must remember, all things can be accomplished in their own time. Our enthusiasm and excitement for our new life is certainly welcome. But we must not forget patience and tolerance. Do I set myself up for failure today?

Higher Power, please grant me the patience and tolerance that I need to manage my pain and my life situations today.

Higher Power, please help me cope with my pain today!

Good morning. Thanks for helping me through the night, it was a rough one. I haven't had that much pain for weeks. Anyway, thanks. I'm grateful to be alive this morning. Would you please watch over me today and help me cope with my pain? You know, it hasn't gone away. Not that I really expected you to take it away, but sometimes I still hope for a miracle.

I haven't asked for anything in quite some time, but today I must. I'm not sure how much more of this pain I can take. I feel my sanity slipping away and hate has begun to replace my love for others. I beg of you to ease my pain today and help me be comfortable with myself and those around me. I know I've never expected this of you before, but today, I must ask. Have I said my prayers to my Higher Power today?

Higher Power, thanks for listening to me and walking beside me today.

Higher Power, please help me cope with my pain today!

42

When we begin our recovery process, we must not get too discouraged when our old instincts or habits reappear. They have been our friends and companions for quite some time. Chances are, we have not yet learned new ways to react to our situations, so we turn to our old instincts for familiar advice and direction.

Some of our instincts and habits of yesterday may apply to managing our pain today and some may not. As we progress in our recovery, we will have an opportunity to form new habits and change those instincts that are no longer needed or useful to managing our pain. This process will demand practice and patience and a whole lot of willingness on our behalf if we are to change and let our new instincts take hold. Do my instincts and habits need changing today?

Higher Power, please grant me the strength and the courage to change those instincts and habits that are harmful to me today.

Higher Power, please help me cope with my pain today!

43

Many of us with chronic pain have asked, "a social life, whats that?" I rarely leave the house anymore and the ones who used to visit have eventually stopped coming for various reasons. My pain has forced me to withdraw from community affairs and I have been left alone. A social life, what's that?

Today it is time to renew our social lives. We can no longer afford to be alone for any length of time with our pain and wallow in self-pity. But if we are to renew our social lives, we must put aside all our excuses and rationales that have kept us in isolation. For some, this may be a difficult and frighting step. Nonetheless it must be taken if we are to break free from our isolation. Today, it is our choice to begin renewing our social life or to remain in our isolation with our pain. Am I comfortable with my social life today?

Higher Power, please help me to begin rebuilding my social life and to become a part of the community again.

Higher Power, please help me cope with my pain today!

44

At one time most of us were prisoners of our pain. We were trapped with no way out and no one around us seemed to know how to help. Society had called out our name, but we could not answer. We were trapped. Our family and friends seemed to carry on without us, stopping once in a while to a faint cry for help. Our world was passing us by. We had become prisoners of our own pain. Am I a prisoner of my pain today?

Higher Power, please set me free today. Show me I no longer need to be a prisoner of my pain.

Higher Power, please help me cope with my pain today!

Taking back our lives today does not mean total freedom from our pain. Nor does it mean freedom from all our difficulties. But it does mean we could quite possibly have freedom from the worst we've experienced. We would no longer need to remain prisoners of our pain and it's despair. We would no longer need to let our pain control our every thought and action. We can come to know peace where there was once despair. We can have faith where there was once hopelessness. Today, we can begin taking our lives back piece by piece and day by day. Today it is our choice. Have I begun taking my life back?

Higher Power, please help me realize the gifts that are awaiting me once I have taken my life back. Grant me the courage to do whatever work is necessary to take my life back today.

Higher Power, please help me cope with my pain today!

At one time or another, most of us have been on our knees in pain crying out for help. We would have done just about anything anyone asked if they would have given us relief from our pain. It wouldn't have mattered who they were or where they had come from. It was help. If we have forgotten about this time in our lives, chances are we have forgotten how to let others extend their hand and help us. Most likely we have become one of those who thinks they can now do everything themselves. Welcoming help has become a thing of the past and pride a thing of the present.

We must remember, we do not have to be on our knees in pain to ask for help today. All that is required from us is the willingness to ask and the willingness to accept. Do I welcome help today?

Higher Power, please help me realize that accepting help from others is not a sign of weakness, but rather a sign of growth.

Higher Power, please help me cope with my pain today!

47

We have every reason in the world to feel sorry for ourselves. Most of us have lost our jobs, material possessions and in some cases ourselves, and were in constant pain. But what good will feeling sorry for ourselves do us? Will it take our pain away or get our job back? NO. Feeling sorry for ourselves will only keep us from moving forward.

We can't afford to feel sorry for ourselves for any length of time. Our new lives are based on gratitude, not self-pity. For us to move forward, take advantage of our new opportunities and manage our pain with any successes, we must rid ourselves of self pity. Am I feeling sorry for myself today?

Higher Power, please replace a feeling of gratitude where I feel self-pity.

Higher Power, please help me cope with my pain today!

Today we are powerless over our pain. We can't control when or where it will surface and in most cases, what the immediate effects will be on us. However, being powerless does not mean total defeat. We may not be able to control when our pain surfaces, but we can control how we react to our pain.

The first step in our recovery is to accept our powerlessness over our initial pain and to realize it is out of our control. Then, and only then, will we be willing to learn how to control our reaction to our pain.

We have a choice today. We can go on thinking that admitting powerlessness is an admission of defeat, or we can use being powerless to our advantage and start managing our pain. Do I think admitting powerlessness over my pain is admitting defeat?

Higher Power, please help me accept my powerlessness over my pain. Please help me realize that I have the power to react positively to my pain and manage it.

Higher Power, please help me cope with my pain today!

Today we are alive. We have not taken our lives, nor have we given ourselves to our pain. Some say they haven't come close to giving up, but others have. Many of us know how close we come to death. We realize that our pain was the pulse of our lives and it could have taken us at any moment, but it didn't.

Today, many of us realize what our pain is capable of doing to us. We realize that managing our pain must be in our hearts at all times. We cannot afford to play roulette here. One shot through the heart so to speak, and the heart of the matter is, we are no more. I am grateful to be alive and well today?

Higher Power, please help me realize the importance of managing my pain today.

Higher Power, please help me cope with my pain today!

I had searched for some time, but never knowing just what it was I was searching for. I have traveled the world over and asked many questions, but received very few answers. One winter day I was introduced to pain and I had many more questions, but very few answers. I began frantically searching as time went on. I wanted something. Some answers. Someone to blame, someone who would understand, or someone to tell me what to do. I don't know. I continued to search and found nothing. Until one day I had looked within. I had found what I had been searching for. It was myself. Have I looked within for my answers today?

Higher Power, please help me begin searching within for my answers today.

Higher Power, please help me cope with my pain today!

Those of us with chronic pain have ended up in some compromising and embarrassing situations in the past and most likely, we will do so in the future. If we don't have a sense of humor today, don't worry, we will have time to work on one.

Today, our greatest roadblock to a sense of humor will be our pride and perfectionism. Most of us want to do everything perfectly and we certainly don't want to look foolish doing it. For us that's almost impossible. We'll never be perfect and having chronic pain, you can bet we will be embarrassed from time to time. Today is our day to find humor with our pain. Can I find some humor with my pain today?

Higher Power, please help me find some humor with my pain today.

Higher Power, please help me cope with my pain today!

Many of us continue hiding in corners like addicts waiting for a quick fix. We're waiting for someone to come by and fix our pain and make us feel like we used to. Some of us may have even traveled from one country to another looking and waiting for someone or something to fix our pain, but we had little success.

Someone stated once, "I was waiting and wondering why *somebody* isn't doing something about my pain, then I realized I was that *somebody*." Today we are responsible for doing what we can to get healthy and manage our pain and if, in the process, someone else fixes it, so be it. But if we continue to wait for this unlikely miracle to occur, we may lose months and possible years, of our lives. Am I waiting for others to fix my pain, or am I taking action towards managing it?

Higher Power, please help me realize that I am the one who is responsible for managing my pain.

Higher Power, please help me cope with my pain today!

For most of us pain relief doesn't come in a bottle, in the shape of a pill, in a powder form or through a needle. These are all just temporary solutions with negative consequences.

Taking drugs may give some temporary relief but as time goes on, we may need to take more and more only to find the effect on our pain becomes less and less. We end up physically and emotionally addicted to our drugs in the process and we are still left with our pain.

Many have screamed out in fear, "You're not taking my drugs away, I can't live with the pain." We understand that fear. We also understand another way, that is the drugs stop here. We urge those of you who want to manage your pain without drugs to seek professional assistance and start on the road to recovery. Have I stopped using drugs as a means of relieving my pain?

Higher Power, please give me the strength and courage to learn how to manage my pain and to not seek relief solely through drugs.

Higher Power, please help me cope with my pain today!

Here comes some pain, quick, call the doctor. Sound familiar? Many of us are too prone to call our doctor when we have a flare-up or set back. We think somehow they will take away our pain and we seem surprised when they respond, "There's nothing I can do." We proceed to get more upset and our pain worsens. If there's nothing our doctor can do for us, and we continue to get upset, why do we continue to call?

Calling our doctor every time we experience pain is not a tool for managing pain. Our freedom from doctors and their freedom from us, starts with working through our pain. Using the tools we have learned and calling others who may give us helpful suggestions is a great place to begin. Calling the doctor every time we have pain will only slow our progress. Do I call the doctor whenever I feel pain?

Higher Power, the next time I have a flare-up or set back, please help me call others who can give me support and suggestions.

Higher Power, please help me cope with my pain today!

Many of us have come to dislike and even hate our bodies. Some of us have become overweight, some have been scarred, and for most of us, our bodies will not do what they were once capable of doing. The good news is, we can work on getting better. The bad news is, if we're not willing to do the work necessary, chances are we won't change. Remember, we can't order a new body. What we have is what we work with. This leaves us with three alternatives: One, we work towards change. Two, we stay the same, or three, we continue to get worse.

We believe if we are to make peace with our bodies we must come to accept them as they are today. Then and only then can we move ahead towards any real change. Today we may not like what we see in the mirror. Our bodies may not look perfect or respond perfectly, but we are who we are and that is what we have to work with today. Have I begun making peace with my body?

Higher Power, please help me learn to accept my body for what it is today. Help me be gentle with myself on my journey to making peace with my body.

Higher Power, please help me cope with my pain today!

The realization of life was not a reality for many of us with chronic pain. We had gone so far down that our comprehension of any life other than one of pain and despair, was unthinkable. We had become convinced that life as we once knew it or wanted it to be was over.

As others began their road to recovery, they had caught a glimpse of the realization of life. They saw others who had chronic pain that seemed to be reasonably content and at peace. They saw others who were living their lives in spite of their pain. What they were seeing was the realization of life working for others who have chronic pain. Do I believe I can live my life in spite of my pain?

Higher Power, please show me the realization of my life today. Please guide me to the road of recovery.

Higher Power, please help me cope with my pain today!

Many times success is based on how much money we have or on the material things we possess or our status within the community. For those of us with chronic pain, success can be defined in terms of our ability to cope with our pain and regain control of our lives. With this definition, we are all successful.

We have turned what seemed to be an impossible situation for us into a new way of living. Some have returned to work, some have gained a better understanding of themselves and others continue to seek out their goals and dreams.

Along our journey, there will be many opportunities for success. They may appear in the form of personal challenges, experiencing a deeper level of spiritual awareness, or even education. Whatever our case may be, we must remember we have already succeeded. For today we have taken back our lives. Do I know I have already succeeded?

Higher Power, please help me realize that taking back my life and coping with pain is the greatest success I can possess.

Higher Power, please help me cope with my pain today!

When a member of the family develops chronic pain, the dynamics of the home usually change. We may have been away for a period of time and now it's time to return home. Upon our arrival we may begin to feel fear and anxiety. Our once secure home may no longer feel safe. Others have taken on our roles. Family members seem to treat us differently. They keep asking us if we're okay or if there is anything they can do for us. This was not the home many of us left or wanted to return to.

For many, coming home will be an adjustment. A time for setting new boundaries, for asking for help, for learning to express our thoughts and feelings, and a time for other family members to adjust to having us back home. Have I shared the responsibility for making my home a safe and secure place to be?

Higher Power, please help me adjust to coming home. Help me to be willing to do my part today and to accept my new role in the home.

Higher Power, please help me cope with my pain today!

For some of us, accepting that we have chronic pain will be the most difficult thing we have ever done. We need to keep in mind that this will be a process and not an event. For some of us acceptance will not be a problem and for others, it will take more time. But it can materialize.

Some believe acceptance means giving up. On the contrary, by accepting we have chronic pain, we are admitting to our condition. That's all. We're not admitting our lives are over or our dreams can no longer be reached. We're saying we need to accept who we are, adjust and move forward. By accepting our condition, we have an opportunity for peace and serenity. Have I accepted that I have chronic pain today?

Higher Power, please grant me the patience and courage to accept I have chronic pain. Help me realize my life is not over, rather it's just begun.

Higher Power, please help me cope with my pain today!

When chronic pain entered our lives they were suddenly turned upside-down and for some, inside-out. What once seemed so clear has become unclear and unpredictable. We have the right to be confused about which direction we should take. However, we can't afford to use our confusion as an excuse to feel sorry for ourselves and do nothing.

Finding a new direction in our life may be confusing at times and at others, we may feel the fear of the unknown. By having patience, willingness, and praying to our Higher Power, our new direction will be revealed, one day at a time. Am I confused about my direction today?

Higher Power, please help guide me in our new direction. Please grant me the patience and willingness to do whatever footwork is necessary along our journey.

Higher Power, please help me cope with my pain today!

Fear will be one of the strongest barriers to our recovery. Most of us at one time have come to know fear in it's most intimate and crippling form. We have feared our pain, our bodies, our actions, ourselves, our futures and much more. We had spent so much time in fear, that we began to wonder if we had come to love it.

In our new life with chronic pain, we will be assured the opportunity of being reintroduced to our fears more than once. Our journey will be filled with the unknown and the unexpected. But we are human and we are sure to be afraid from time to time. This is certainly normal. But to continue to love our fear is not. Today, we must begin our separation from the love we may hold for our fear and begin a new relationship with faith. Am I consumed by fear today or have I chosen to seek faith?

Higher Power, please help me cast aside my fear and begin seeking faith.

Higher Power, please help me cope with my pain today!

Many of us would rather forget our past. We would rather forget the day we were injured or the fight we have fought to arrive where we are today. We would rather forget the pain and the broken relationships. We would rather forget how angry we had become and how our depression had dictated our lives. For many of us this was our past and we wanted it put to rest.

However painful our past experiences have been for us, we must not forget them. Remembering where we have come from will be our guide for the future and a block to returning to our past. Remember, experience is our best teacher and best remembered. Do I remember my past or have I tried to forget it?

Higher Power, please help me realize that my past is not to be forgotten.

Higher Power, please help me cope with my pain today!

We awoke this morning to the same pain as yesterday. Our attempt to drown our pain in alcohol yesterday had failed once again. But with little or no conscious effort we began drinking again, hoping that this time we would be successful. We were sure we could drink our pain away. Besides everything else we had tried seemed to make our pain worse. This had to work.

The day grew worse and the night came. We were once again unsuccessful. Our pain was wiser and stronger than alcohol. We felt complete defeat and hopelessness, for what we thought would work had failed us. As we slipped into the night we found ourselves praying. We asked our Higher Power to direct us to a place or person that could help us cope with our pain, because our way had surely proven to be the wrong way. Do I use mood-altering chemicals to cope with my pain?

Higher Power, please show me another way of coping with my pain.

Higher Power, please help me cope with my pain today!

MARCH

A man asked his friend one day to scold him if he did one more thing wrong during that day. His friend replied "No. You're doing a better job than I could ever do." The man's friend was right. We rarely give ourselves a break. Yet many times we will give others a break for making the same mistake we have often punished ourselves for making.

It is time we learn to give ourselves a break. To join the ranks of the forgiving. It is time to live and let live. We are nowhere near perfect and to pretend that we are, is an injustice to our humanity. Today it is our choice. We can continue punishing ourselves for being human and making mistakes or we can begin to forgive ourselves as others do. Do I give myself a break today?

Higher Power, please show me that I don't have to do everything perfectly. Teach me how to give myself a well deserved break today.

Higher Power, please help me cope with my pain today!

We can hold our head high for we haven't given up. We have faced adversity and continue to face adversity like no others have. We have fought through days of pain hoping and praying the next would be better. For some, we have entered into a new life and faced it with courage and honesty. For others, we have returned to our previous lives only to be questioned and talked about.

Whatever adversity we have faced, we can be proud of who we are and where we have come from. To not give up and to keep striving for a better tomorrow, is the hardest and most noble work we can ever perform. For that alone, we can hold our heads high. Can I hold my head high or am I embarrassed and ashamed of who I am?

Higher Power, please help me accept who I am and where I have come from. Please help me hold my head high, for I am who I am.

Higher Power, please help me cope with my pain today!

There may be a better way of living with our pain. It may not be an easier, softer way or a way that we would have chosen, but it is another way. It's a way of living that demands our recovery be our first priority. A way of living that demands we seek spiritual growth each day. That we come to believe in a power greater than ourselves. A way of living that keeps us in today. A way that we refrain from dwelling on what we used to be like or what we think we may become. A way of living that is one of giving of ourselves rather than seeking personal gains. It will be a way of living where we have come to accept ourselves for who we are today. Do I know there may be a better way for me?

Higher Power, thank you for showing me a better way to live.

Higher Power, please help me cope with my pain today!

One prescription for healing and taking our mind off our pain is laughter. When we think back to the last time we really laughed, chances are we remember feeling good inside and experiencing minimal pain. If we can't feel those things today, chances are we need a dose of laughter.

In time we will not only be healing our souls and paying less attention to our pain, we will also be learning how to take life less seriously. We will come to know humor where there was once pain and healing where there was bitterness. Have I discovered what laughter can do for me?

Higher Power, please help me find humor in my life today.

Higher Power, please help me cope with my pain today!

There are days many of us wonder why we should get out of bed at all. Our pain is at an all time high and we are at odds with ourselves and the world around us. Our serenity and peace of mind seem nonexistent. Our attitude fades to one of, who cares.

These days are meant for hanging on. If all our attempts to rectify our situations and our attitude have failed, it may be our time to hang on and be content with doing the best we can. We needn't be concerned with our list of things to do for the day or run a guilt trip on ourselves for hours on end. The fact is, some days are meant for just hanging on. Do I know what days are meant for hanging on and which aren't?

Higher Power, help me accept that there may be days when all I can do is hang on.

Higher Power, please help me cope with my pain today!

What is this pain management stuff anyway? Some may have tried it for days, weeks and maybe months and they feel worse than before. Those who feel this way may want to reconsider your options and give managing your pain another chance. Learning how to manage our pain doesn't come overnight. Nor does the body respond to our efforts overnight. This is a process that takes time to learn and adapt to. It takes practice, successes, failures, and a ton of patience. Remember, our lives could be at risk. Have I given managing my pain a chance today?

Higher Power, please grant me the patience to manage my pain today. Help me realize that my life may depend on it.

Higher Power, please help me cope with my pain today!

When is someday? Is it today? Was it yesterday? Is it tomorrow or is it next year? Someday can be any day we want it to be. If we don't want it to be, someday doesn't have to come at all. Someday could be the day we begin managing our pain or someday could be the day we decide we can no longer continue on.

Someday has to be a day that we choose. It's the day we decide to take action on whatever we have been telling ourselves we would do if and when that someday ever came. For some, their someday would never arrive. Their pain and despair had won over them. For the rest of us, our someday is today. Is my someday today?

Higher Power, please take away my procrastination and help me do today what I have been thinking about doing on that someday that hasn't arrived.

Higher Power, please help me cope with my pain today!

Before our pain entered our lives, most of us have felt inadequate at one time or another. But that day our pain took over our lives, was the day we would truly come to know the meaning of feeling inadequate.

Most of us no longer felt we were capable of doing the task at hand. We began feeling like we had failed. We began comparing ourselves with our peers, hoping we would find someone we could measure up to. But most of us had little success. We were left with our pain and our feelings of inadequacies.

As our recovery progresses, we will be presented with the choice of continuing to compare ourselves to others or to begin focusing on the capabilities we possess and begin confronting the inadequacies that lie within. Do I hide my inadequacies today?

Higher Power, help me face my inadequacies today.

Higher Power, please help me cope with my pain today!

When we were in our depths of despair, most of us swore we had lost any peace of mind we may have had. Some of us swore we had lost our minds entirely and we questioned whether or not we would ever experience peace and contentment again.

As we progress in our recovery many of us have come to find that our Higher Power is restoring our peace of mind, piece by piece. For some, this restoration will be swift and painless. For others, it may take some time and effort but it is near and it can materialize. Do I believe peace of mind is near for me?

Higher Power, today I am willing to do whatever is asked of me to find and keep what peace of mind you are willing to give me.

Higher Power, please help me cope with my pain today!

After our injuries, most of us had come to feel uncomfortable and somewhat confused about our sexuality. What once seemed fine, was now haunted by uncertainty and questions of doubt. We wondered if we would re-injure ourselves if we had attempted to do what once seemed so natural. We wondered what our partner would think and how they may respond. But most of all, we wondered if we were really ready for this.

We cannot answer these questions for anyone. What we can say is that we must address any inadequacies and confusion we may have before moving forward. If questions and inadequacies still remain, chances are it is not our time. Do I feel comfortable with my sexuality today?

Higher Power, please help me take all the time that I need to become comfortable with my feelings and attitudes towards my sexuality today.

Higher Power, please help me cope with my pain today!

In order for those of us with chronic pain to avoid returning to the physical and emotional despair we come from, we must begin practicing regular daily maintenance on ourselves. We can't afford to let our bodies deteriorate to the point they were when we were inactive. Nor can we let our psychological self fall to the dangers of the insanity and depression we had come to know so well in the beginning.

Maintenance for us means doing regular exercise, keeping our feelings and attitudes in check, and of course daily prayer and meditation. Whatever maintenance program we choose to follow in our recovery, it must be done daily. Without maintenance, we are sure to begin slipping backwards and for some, we may not have another chance to return. Do I practice a daily maintenance program today?

Higher Power, please give me the strength to apply whatever maintenance I may need to manage my pain today.

Higher Power, please help me cope with my pain today!

The true purpose of a chronic pain support group is for us to share our experiences, strengths, and hopes with each other. They are not for us to fulfill our dating desires with the newcomer to our meeting. The newcomer who comes to the group is feeling just as lonely and scared as we were in the beginning. They want our support and friendship, not pressures.

When we express anything other than genuineness, we have put the newcomer, the group, and ourselves at risk of failing our true purpose. Do I know the appropriate way to share myself at support groups?

Higher Power, please help me share my experience, strengths, and hopes with the newcomer today.

Higher Power, please help me cope with my pain today!

We must never forget where we came from and what we were like when we first needed help. We were emotionally, physically and spiritually ill. There were no up days, just down ones. As time passed, our days shifted to ones of ups and downs. One day we feel better physically but emotionally we're down. The next day we feel better emotionally but down physically. Somehow we have caught the ups and downs.

At this point, many of us begin to wonder if there is such a thing as a balance. Yes there is.

For some it will come quickly and for others, it may take more time to materialize. Eventually our ups and downs can be replaced by calmness and balance. Have I reached some sort of calmness and balance in my life?

Higher Power, please help me through my times of ups and downs. Please help me realize I too can find calmness and balance in my life.

Higher Power, please help me cope with my pain today!

Whether we have back pain, leg pain, headaches, pain from surgery or pain from cancer, it is all the same. It is pain. Sometimes it's forgiving, sometimes unforgiving.

When we start comparing who has traveled the rougher road or who has the most pain, we either want others to feel sorry for us or we are feeding our egos. This type of behavior is dangerous. It only blocks our chances for growth and managing our pain. Today we can continue to have others feel sorry for us or feed our egos, or we can use our experiences to benefit ourselves and others. Do I realize my pain is the same as others but my experiences may be different?

Higher Power, please help me realize that pain is the same for us all. It is pain.

Higher Power, please help me cope with my pain today!

Pain is our silent and seemingly invisible partner. No one can hear our silent partner, nor can they see it. Others have said that once we become friends with our silent partner, we will begin to understand it's silence. We will come to know when our partner is angry and what effects it may inflict on us. Sometimes we will know when it will occur and other times it will be a surprise. It is said that our silent partner will be ours for life and that it is in our best interest to become true friends with it. We know you would rather not, but you have little choice. For today, our silent partner is our pain. Do I know who my silent partner is?

Higher Power, please help me become friends with my silent partner so I may manage it rather than it managing me.

Higher Power, please help me cope with my pain today!

Many of us in the beginning have a difficult time focusing our thoughts. We had immediately concluded we were losing our minds. Don't panic, this is normal. Our focus has been our pain and despair. Nothing else. For some our focus may be blurred by depression. Again don't panic. Most of us are restored to clear thinking and can return to our work or other activities.

When we begin to manage our pain and our depression subsides, our thoughts will no longer be all consuming as they once were. We will begin to focus on the tasks at hand. Remember, this can take time. It is a process, not an event. Chances are we will not be successful overnight. With practice and patience we can once again begin focusing our thoughts. Are my thoughts focused on my pain or on my tasks at hand?

Higher Power, please help me refocus my thoughts today.

Higher Power, please help me cope with my pain today!

Before starting our day, we can be calm and think of the twenty-four hours that lie ahead. We can ask our Higher Power for the strength to manage our pain. We can ask for acceptance to live within our limitations for this day. We can ask that our Higher Power's will be done and not ours. We can ask that our Higher Power help us grow spiritually rather than seeking self-reliance. We can ask that our Higher Power take away any defects that we may have which stand in our way of helping others for this day. We can ask this of our Higher Power by praying in the morning. Do I pray before the start of each day?

Higher Power, please help me realize that you are there each morning for me and all that I need to do, is pray.

Higher Power, please help me cope with my pain today!

When we lose someone or something or have it taken away from us, we are sure to experience some type of grief. Those of us with chronic pain have either had a sudden injury or a progressive illness that has created a loss in our lives. Some of us have lost a career, our mobility, our identity, and some have lost their previous way of life. It is like we have lost our best friend.

Each of us with chronic pain will have our own issues relating to grief and loss. What remains the same is that we must not forget or deny ourselves the opportunity to go through our grieving process. Without forgiveness and acceptance we are sure to remain spiteful towards our situations and ourselves. Have I allowed myself to grieve over my losses?

Higher Power, please grant me the courage to face whatever feelings of loss I may have in my life today.

Higher Power, please help me cope with my pain today!

Many of us at one time or another have fallen to our knees and asked our Higher Power to ease our pain. Yet for many of us, this hasn't happened. What we may have forgotten is that we are responsible for doing the footwork. If we want to learn how to manage our pain, we must play an active role. It's quite simple. We get out of it what we put into it. If we expect others to do our work they will reap the rewards, not us. For our best chances of success, we must begin doing the footwork and leave the results to our Higher Power. Have I begun doing the footwork that is needed to manage my pain today or do I expect others to do the work for me?

Higher Power, please give me the strength to do whatever footwork is asked of me today. Help me have faith that the results are in your hands.

Higher Power, please help me cope with my pain today!

So many of us have said, "It's their fault I'm like this," or "There has to be someone I can blame for what has happened to me." True. If we look hard enough we can lay the blame on someone. But will that reverse what has happened to us or help us feel any better about ourselves? Chances are it won't. All blaming others accomplishes is it causes us to resent others and to deny us from looking inward.

When we're compelled and consumed with the need to blame someone, we become bitter and angry people. We begin to see the world as a place of right and wrong and not one of indifferences. Today, we must stop blaming others and begin taking responsibility for ourselves. Today, it's not who can I blame, but how can I look within for my answers. Have I stopped blaming others for my injury and my pain?

Higher Power, please help me begin to look within myself for my answers and to stop blaming others.

Higher Power, please help me cope with my pain today!

Why have I chosen a life of recovery from chronic pain? We all know that this is the road less traveled, yet we've chosen it. Most of us have fantasized about an easier, softer way at one time or another, yet we chose the road less traveled. Many have asked themselves if they would have learned the lessons they have or found themselves again if they had chosen a different way. Most likely not.

With our choice, we will come to realize that any other way of coping with our pain would not suffice. There are no easier, softer ways that have been found that produce the same results as taking the road less traveled. Have I chosen the road less traveled or am I searching for an easier, softer, way?

Higher Power, please guide me and stand by my side as I take the road less traveled.

Higher Power, please help me cope with my pain today!

In the beginning, many of us didn't have to look too far within ourselves to find hatred. It seems for those of us with chronic pain, it has become easier to find hatred and fault than it has to find the gratitude that lies within. As our recoveries progressed, some have found their gratitude that lies within, but others are not as fortunate. They remain full of blame and hatred. Their focus remains on what they are no longer able to do rather than on what they are capable of doing today. This type of attitude is sure to keep us hateful rather than grateful.

Today is our day for transformation. It is a day we can leave behind the hate that has shadowed the gratitude that lies within. It is a day we can begin being grateful for what we have and not hateful for what we may have lost. Am I grateful or hateful today?

Higher Power, please show me how much I have to feel grateful for today.

Higher Power, please help me cope with my pain today!

Special crazy days are days that belong to us. They are the days when we think our pain is worse than anyone else's and whatever goes wrong, it happens to us. This is our special crazy day. It is a day for us to simply survive. A day to find humor in, to get upset with, to cry over, and to wish that it would just go away.

When our special day comes, we must keep in mind that we are only human. We must keep it all in prospective. Above all we should smile and say, "This is my crazy day and it too shall pass." Can I remember what it takes to get through my special crazy day?

Higher Power, please help me smile and keep a positive attitude on my special crazy day.

Higher Power, please help me cope with my pain today!

Today we start our new journey towards managing our pain and finding our way. A journey towards acceptance of a Higher Power and of ourselves. A journey towards a better tomorrow. A journey that will help us find our way.

Some of us will stumble and fall along the way, while others will have little resistance. Some will accept their new way and others will continue to fight and demand they have everything their way, while others will insist that they be shown their way immediately.

Our journey towards finding our way will be just that. A journey. A process that will present opportunities for growth and change. When we become patient and listen for direction from our Higher Power, we will find our way. Have I started my new journey towards finding my way?

Higher Power, please direct me on my journey towards finding my way.

Higher Power, please help me cope with my pain today!

Many of us who are single and have chronic pain have desperately shouted out, "my life is over. I'm sure to live the rest of my days alone. Who would want me when they have all those others without pain and imperfections to choose from." This could be true, but it's highly unlikely.

When we are ready, we will be introduced to that someone special, who will accept us as we are and not for who we may become. In the mean time, we can take advantage of the time we have and work on our recovery and patiently wait for that special someone. Do I feel sorry for myself and think that no one will love me because of my pain?

Higher Power, I know there is a reason for my situation today. Please help me have patience and help me accept that when I am ready, that special someone will be put in my life.

Higher Power, please help me cope with my pain today!

91

I awake to my pain as I did yesterday and the day before that. I pour a cup of coffee. I begin to realize I have a full day ahead of me and that the pain I had yesterday will be my companion for today. I tell myself that I survived quite well yesterday and I'm sure I will do the same today. I pour another cup of coffee and I am suddenly reminded that my companion has awoken and is ready for the day. As I begin walking out the door, I had found myself saying, "are you coming? We are companions for today you know." What messages do I tell myself about my pain in the morning?

Higher Power, please help me keep a positive attitude about my pain today.

Higher Power, please help me cope with my pain today!

We may not have the power to take away one hundred percent of our pain, but we do possess the power to reduce our pain and it's effects. This is known as managing our pain. It is the ability we have to bring about change and the way we react to our pain, so we may lead a full and productive lifestyle. This concept alone is useless without our participation. We are in charge of using our powers; not the doctors, our spouses, or our friends. Our powers are ours and it is up to us to use them accordingly.

Finding and learning how to use the powers within may take time to develop. There will be times of triumphs and times of disappointments. But eventually we will have learned how to reduce, manage, and live with our pain. Have I discovered that I have the power to reduce the pain within me?

Higher Power, please help me find whatever powers I may have to reduce my pain today and please show me how the use them.

Higher Power, please help me cope with my pain today!

Many of us find ourselves becoming impatient when it comes to wanting answers about our new direction. We have asked many difficult questions about our lives, yet we expect definite answers immediately. We must remain patient. Our direction has yet to be determined by our Higher Power. But when it is, we will be the first to know.

When we remain impatient and become demanding we have decreased our chances of finding our new direction. We have told our Higher Power that we know better. We are in charge and we no longer have faith in anyone or anybody but ourselves. When we become impatient for direction, we must take to our knees and pray to the only one who really knows the fate of our direction and ask for the patience that we so desperately need. Am I impatient about my direction today?

Higher Power, please take away my impatience today. Help me have faith that whatever direction you have for me will be the one I will take.

Higher Power, please help me cope with my pain today!

Some say we can't go on to the future until we have dealt with our past. This is especially true for those of us with chronic pain. For some of us, our pain was thrust upon us without warning. For others, our pain has been a slow progression. Whatever our case, we need an accurate account of what our lives were like before we were injured. Then we need to know what happened to us. From these accounts our questions of the past may be answered.

Many of our conflicts today can stem from the experiences surrounding our injury. Our present anger, resentments, depression and so forth, can all be linked to our past. By taking an accurate account of these facts, we will be able to piece together what has happened in our lives, strive for acceptance and then begin to move towards the future. Have I taken an accurate look at my past?

Higher Power, please give me the courage to look to my past for answers, not excuses.

Higher Power, please help me cope with my pain today!

Setting goals will become extremely important in our recovery. Those of us with chronic pain have had periods of time where we were imprisoned by our pain and we were unable to set goals, let alone pursue them. Our ambitions, our goals and our dreams had been temporarily taken away.

As our recovery progresses, we will discover there will be new goals to set and new challenges to meet. Some will find themselves pursuing past goals, while others have accepted they can no longer accomplish what they once could. Whatever our case may be, it is time we put our fears aside and let ambition and enthusiasm take hold and begin setting goals. Am I setting goals for myself today?

Higher Power, please help me begin setting reasonable goals for myself today.

Higher Power, please help me cope with my pain today!

As spring approaches, many of us are beginning to make plans for long overdue projects and fun. Our enthusiasm for life is running high and we can't wait to get started. But before we proceed, we must remember how we arrived at where we are. We have paced ourselves. We have given ourselves the care we have needed, and the ability to not let our lives become unmanageable.

We have made plans one day at a time and we haven't forgotten who and what we are and where we have come from. Nor have we forgotten what our responsibilities are towards our recovery. The months ahead can be filled with fun and joy, providing we remember and practice what we have learned. Have I learned to pace myself today?

Higher Power, please help me learn how to pace myself today and for the months ahead.

Higher Power, please help me cope with my pain today!

APRIL

Many of us with chronic pain have either know-ingly or unknowingly developed selective listening. We hear what we want and when we want and in some cases, we carefully twist other's words to fit what we want to hear. When others told us our pain was not going to go away, many of us had interpreted that to mean someone could cure us. Some of us attentively listened while others gave suggestions on managing our pain, but somehow we heard this did not apply to us. We were hearing what we wanted to hear.

In the beginning this is quite normal. But as our recovery progresses, selective listening can be danger-ous. Listening to what we tell ourselves and what others are really saying to us, may be difficult at first. We understand that truth and reality can be painful and hard to accept especially when we have other ideas. Do I have selective listening today?

Higher Power, as painful as truth and reality may be at times, please help me hear the truth from myself and others today.

Higher Power, please help me cope with my pain today!

Those of us with chronic pain have either knowingly or unknowingly, learned how to respond to our pain. We make subtle sounds such as moans, and groans, and of course, the ouches. We have gone to great lengths to make sure that we and those around us, know we are in pain. All we have really accomplished by this behavior is, we have kept ourselves prisoners of our pain and we have invited others to feel sorry for us.

Part of managing our pain today means managing our responses to our pain. Unlearning what we have become so familiar with will take patience, an awareness of our behavior, and the willingness to give up the attention our responses have brought us. How do I respond to my pain today?

Higher Power, please help me learn to express my pain in a healthy way today.

Higher Power, please help me cope with my pain today!

We who have chronic pain know what it is like to lose parts of our self-esteem in the blink of an eye. For some of us, our pain had suddenly taken away what we were once able to do and the positive feelings we had about ourselves, only to be replaced by self-doubt, hatred, and self-pity. We no longer had felt good about ourselves or what we were or were not able to do. Our purpose for ourselves and our families and our lives in general, had vanished.

If we are to rebuild our self-esteem today, we must first begin learning how to manage our pain. Without a firm hold on our pain, it has the power to take away any progress we may have made. We must remember, rebuilding our self-esteem will be a process and it cannot be done overnight. Nor can we do it alone. We must ask our Higher Power for the strength, the courage and the guidance to search within for the self-esteem our pain had once taken away. How is my self-esteem today?

Higher Power, please grant me the courage to improve my self-esteem each day.

Higher Power, please help me cope with my pain today!

Accepting the help of others has been a dilemma for many of us with chronic pain. We either let them do it all for us or we've taken it all upon ourselves. We either think we are incapable of doing anything, or if we accept the help of others, we are in some way incapable and weak people.

In our recovery, it is important that we find a balance between accepting and declining help from others. We can no longer afford to let others do all our work, nor can we afford to try and do it all ourselves. Either way, we must remember there are consequences. Do I accept a little help from my friends today?

Higher Power, please help me put aside my pride and my fear so that I may take responsibility for my part and let my friends offer a little help.

Higher Power, please help me cope with my pain today!

When we follow the principles of managing our pain, it is like taking out an insurance policy on our lives. These principles are W.O.P.S.: Willingness, Open-mindedness, Patience, and Slips.

Willingness stands for how far we are willing to go and what risks we are willing to take to stay healthy and grow.

Open-mindedness is just that. To keep an open mind at all times and to explore all possibilities.

Patience means learning that everything won't come at once. Some things take time and by practicing patience we will allow these things to materialize.

Slips are what we have when we forget to work the rest of the principles. We slip back to the physical and emotional pain we so desperately wanted out of. Do I practice these principles when managing my pain?

Higher Power, please give me the willingness and courage to practice these principles today.

Higher Power, please help me cope with my pain today!

Most of us play the "if" game and we're not even aware of it. We say things like, "If only my pain would go away," or "If only I hadn't been injured," or "If only they understood," and on and on. In this context, "if" is a wish that rarely materializes. Chances are, our pain won't disappear and the fact that we were injured cannot be changed.

When we live our lives by "ifs," we are not living life on life's terms. We are living our lives on conditions we have set that rarely materialize. As a result, we begin to feel sorry for ourselves and wonder, "what if". Am I living life on life's terms today or do I wonder "what if"?

Higher Power, please help me live my life on life's terms today. Help me take responsibility for myself and stop playing the "if" game.

Higher Power, please help me cope with my pain today!

Many of us with chronic pain have come to the conclusion that if we are no longer able to do what we used to do, we can no longer do anything at all. If this is our belief, our lives are sure to be filled with boredom and our hopes and dreams are sure to fade away.

Having chronic pain is not a permanent license to stay bored. Rather it is a license to change direction and begin a new life. If we are bored today, chances are we haven't changed our direction or our attitudes. Each and every one of us has our special gifts. They may be from our past or ones we have yet to discover. Chances are if we are bored today, it isn't because we are no longer capable of doing, rather it is because we are not doing. Am I bored today?

Higher Power, please help me change my direction today. Help me change those attitudes that keep me prisoner of my own boredom.

Higher Power, please help me cope with my pain today!

Those of us with chronic pain know what it is like to dislike parts of ourselves. The day that pain invaded our bodies was a day many of us would remember as the day we no longer liked ourselves. For many, this day would turn into weeks, months and years. We had come to believe that as long as we had pain and it's symptoms, we couldn't possibly like ourselves.

We started believing that others could never like us or even begin to accept us with all our imperfections. We had become prisoners of our pain and it's emotional turmoil. Liking ourselves at this point had seemed almost impossible. What many of us had failed to accept about ourselves, had become our enemy and would keep us from liking ourselves. Do I like myself today?

Higher Power, please help me learn to accept and like myself for who I am today.

Higher Power, please help me cope with my pain today!

Countless times many of us have said, "I don't care. I can't stand the pain anymore. I don't want to go on living like this. I'm never going to get better." Sound familiar? Chances are it does.

Those of us with chronic pain play a tape to ourselves called "I don't care." It is usually played when our pain is out of control or when our lives are in some kind of turmoil. Most of the times we scream out "I don't care," it is out of frustration and a plea for help. But deep down most of us do care. It's just that we're not always able to say, "I do care." Do I mean it when I say "I don't care?"

Higher Power, please help me find and keep that part of me that does care.

Higher Power, please help me cope with my pain today!

"God grant me the serenity to accept the things I cannot change, the courage to change the things I can, and the wisdom to know the difference." This well known prayer has made a difference in millions of people's lives and for those of us with chronic pain, this prayer will become our savior.

Whatever situation we may find ourselves in, or however much pain and confusion we have, we can pause and say the Serenity Prayer to ourselves. We can ask our Higher Power to grant us the serenity and the acceptance and the courage to cope with the situation at hand. The results of this prayer will become our peace and our guidance. Do I take time out during my day to say the Serenity Prayer?

Higher Power, please teach me to take a moment or two each day to pray for serenity, courage and wisdom.

Higher Power, please help me cope with my pain today!

Many of us with chronic pain have fought the battle of our lives to reach this point in our recovery. But for some, their battle is far from over. Their days continue to be filled with darkness and their nights seem endless. They have yet to see the sunlight, just darkness.

For some their bed remains their domain. They remain prisoners of their pain and depression. Their emotional pain and turmoil has held back every attempt to search for the sunlight. Their outlook on life has faded to one of hopelessness. Their pain and despair was winning their battle.

We know that rising to one's feet again is not an easy process. We understand that it will take all the faith and courage we can possibly muster to break free. But we also realize that eventually our endless nights can fade and our darkened days can shift to sunlight. Can I see the sunlight today?

Higher Power, help he overcome the darkness of my days and my endless nights. Help me to see the sunlight today.

Higher Power, please help me cope with my pain today!

111

For the first time, many of us are learning how to cope with and express our feelings. For those of us with chronic pain, the feeling we need to be most concerned with in the beginning, is anger. Most of us had stuffed our anger from the day of our injury. Some were not sure how to safely express it, while others had felt if they had come to terms with their anger, it was a sure admission to their situation.

Whatever our case may be, we must remember unresolved anger is serious business. In the fraction of a second we can become rageful and out of control or prolonged over a period of time, our anger can lead to serious depression. Either way it is unresolved anger and it is unwanted and unwarranted. Do I have unresolved anger today?

Higher Power, please help me realize what my unresolved anger is today and to take action to resolve it.

Higher Power, please help me cope with my pain today!

In the beginning of our recovery, most of us will experience highs and lows with our emotions. Don't panic. This is to be expected. There are many issues we have yet to sort out. Many of us find it almost impossible just trying to cope with the highs and lows that accompany our pain.

This is a time to be gentle and forgiving with ourselves. There is no perfect way to cope with our highs and lows and the feelings we have. With time, prayer and patience, we will have an opportunity to resolve our issues. Until then, it is our attitude and our Higher Power that will help us through this time of highs and lows. How am I managing my highs and lows today?

Higher Power, please guide me through this time of highs and lows. Help me realize that in time I will reach a balance with my highs and lows.

Higher Power, please help me cope with my pain today!

We will come to realize after attempting to manage our pain, that an attitude of, "I must do it right or else", will not suffice. All we can do is try. Nothing more nothing less. When we attach right and wrong to managing our pain, we have set ourselves up and given ourselves permission to give up without even trying.

All that is asked of us today is to put our best foot forward. To truly know that we have given all possibilities a sincere effort. This however does not guarantee every effort we put forth will have a successful outcome. But this must not stop us from continuing to try. We must remember today, that if we do not try we are sure to accomplish nothing. Do I keep trying each day?

Higher Power, please give me the courage to try regardless of what I think the outcome may be.

Higher Power, please help me cope with my pain today!

Our pain in some direct or indirect way has taken away the quality of our lives. When we began managing our pain, many of us decided we wanted to get back what we had lost and more. We no longer wanted quality. We wanted quantity.

Even if we had the capabilities to put forth the effort and retrieve what we have lost, what would the quality of our life be like in the process? Most likely we wouldn't have much time for our family or friends. Nor would we spend much time on improving ourselves. We would be so focused on getting back what we had lost that our lives are no longer one of quality and contentment, but rather one of quantity and emptiness. Is my life one of quality or quantity today?

Higher Power, please help me begin living a life of quality and not one of quantity.

Higher Power, please help me cope with my pain today!

Having chronic pain, we know that many of our slips are unavoidable. Our bodies have their own intentions and they usually carry them out. However there are slips that can be avoided. These are the ones that we bring about ourselves. They usually happen when we begin neglecting our recovery.

Our slips begin when other areas of our lives have taken priority over our recovery. When our exercise program had shifted to the couch and we lose sight of ourselves physically and spiritually we have begun slipping backwards. We have allowed ourselves the opportunity to return to that place we so desperately wanted to leave.

If we are to avoid slipping backwards today, we must begin changing our priorities and our attitudes. Our recovery must be a priority in our lives and we must make a commitment to begin avoiding those slips that can be avoided. Do I bring about the slips I have in my life today?

Higher Power, please help me see the difference between avoidable and unavoidable slips today. Help me avoid slipping back to where I once came from.

Higher Power, please help me cope with my pain today!

Do you believe having chronic pain is a life and death situation for some? Do you believe others have taken their own lives while in extreme pain and emotional turmoil? Do you believe depression, whether mild or severe is a symptom of chronic pain? Do you believe some of us with chronic pain have turned to alcohol and drugs in search of relief from our pain? Do you believe some of us continually view ourselves as victims of society? Do you believe chronic pain has aided in the destruction of families and has caused many personal relationships to cease? What do you believe? Do I believe having chronic pain can do any of this to me?

Higher Power, please help me realize the capabilities of chronic pain. Help me realize that without working at recovery each day, these and many other consequences could occur in my life.

Higher Power, please help me cope with my pain today!

There are many who suffer needlessly from chronic pain each day. They have yet to discover that there is a way of managing their pain and a way they can climb up from their depths of despair. There are many who have yet to find their home. To that place where they can learn to manage their pain. To that place where others understand us and where we have been and that will love us unconditionally. To them we say "there is such a peace and it is waiting just for you."

For those of us who have found our way home we are the fortunate ones. We have found what others desperately want and have been searching for. If we are to keep what we have been so fortunate to find, we must help the others who continue to struggle to find their way home—to that place where they feel they belong. Have I found a place where I feel I belong today?

Higher Power, please lift me from my depths of my pain and suffering and show me to the place I belong.

Higher Power, please help me cope with my pain today!

With chronic pain we can't be sure of what our pain will be like from day to day. We can have a good day, a good week, a good month, or even several good months in a row. Unfortunately the opposite is true as well. With chronic pain we will inevitability have our not so good days.

On these days, it is important that we look back to the good days and weeks we have had and remember just how we felt about ourselves and our lives in general. Chances are, we were happy and content. This is what we can draw from on our not so good days. We can seek that hope and encouragement, but most of all, we can remember that it is okay to have our not so good days and that they too shall soon pass. Do I accept my good days and not so good days?

Higher Power, please help me accept and learn from both my good days and my not so good days.

Higher Power, please help me cope with my pain today!

119

We have come from the depths of despair into a new life. We have been chosen as the ones to survive. We were the hopeless ones that many had written off. We are now the miracles. Serenity, courage, and wisdom are becoming a part of our lives. Day by day we are collecting the blessings of life.

If we are having troubles seeing our blessings and finding a miracle today, look in the mirror and you will surely find one. Have I collected my blessings today?

Higher Power, please help me collect my blessing for today and help me see that I am truly a miracle.

Higher Power, please help me cope with my pain today!

As our recovery progressed, we realized we had been neglecting and in some cases, purposefully avoiding many areas of our lives that needed attention. Some had thought managing our pain was all that was required or that by managing our pain, the rest of our lives would come about. While others had known there was work to be done, they came to the conclusion it was simply too much work or too great of a risk to be taken.

Whatever our position may be today, the fact is, there is work to be done. Coping with chronic pain and becoming healthier will require a holistic approach. We must strive to improve our physical, emotional, and spiritual conditions daily. Our attitude of too much work on our behalf or if I see nothing, I do nothing will not suffice. If we are to become healthy today we must begin doing the work that is needed. Am I on my way to becoming healthier?

Higher Power, please show me what areas of my life need my attention today.

Higher Power, please help me cope with my pain today!

Today, our Higher Power is leading us towards the unexpected. It could be to a place, to a relationship, towards the awareness and use of a hidden talent, or even towards a life of peace and contentment. Whatever it may be, we are being prepared each and every day to expect the unexpected.

Expecting the unexpected today is not about our selfishness and our masterful plans. Rather it is about hope and faith. It is the understanding that those of us who have chronic pain can and have an opportunity to experience all that life has to offer. It is the belief that our Higher Power is in charge of our direction and to expect anything short of the unexpected or a miracle would be a lack of faith on our behalf.

When the time has arrived to expect the unexpected we will know. Whatever it may be, it will not be by our own doing, but by our Higher Power. Have I come to believe in and expect the unexpected in my life?

Higher Power, please help me be patient and prepare myself for whatever unexpected gifts you may bring to me today.

Higher Power, please help me cope with my pain today!

What happens to those of us with chronic pain as we get older? Does our injury grow worse? Will we have more pain? Will we be able to work? Will we even be able to get out of bed? The answer to these and many other questions we may have is, we don't know. Yet many of us spend countless hours in turmoil worrying about what has yet to happen.

We understand the magnitude of these questions and their outcomes. But we also know, that by projecting and in some cases, living in the future, we are neglecting to live in today. We are wasting the very life we have today for one we have little or no control over. Am I dwelling on getting older and having more pain or do I live my life one day at a time?

Higher Power, please help me realize that worrying about the future will only stop me from living today.

Higher Power, please help me cope with my pain today!

123

Most of us are not the same as we once were physically. As a result, we have come to know a new word. Limitations. It has become the least talked about word with some and others have come to know their own definition and it's boundaries.

Learning to accept we can no longer do some of the things we once could and that there may be restrictions on what we can do in the future, has become devastating for many. Some have cried out, "I can't accept this. I won't. There has to be another way." Sorry, we have yet to find another way except through the acceptance of our condition.

We know this will be one of the most difficult things to accept and abide by in our recovery. But we also know through this acceptance, we will have an opportunity to know ourselves as never before. We will discover hidden desires, passions, and talents that will become the directors of our new lives. Have I accepted my limitations today?

Higher Power, please help me come to accept my limitations and to begin using them to move forward in my recovery.

Higher Power, please help me cope with my pain today!

The fear of re-injury lurks within most of us. It is a reality that cannot be disputed. But some of us take this fear to the extreme. We let this fear run our lives and in turn we forget to live them. Some are truly afraid of re-injuring themselves, while others have knowingly or unknowingly used this fear as an excuse not to try. Consequently, we remain stagnant in our recovery.

A healthy fear of re-injuring ourselves and an awareness of our body and it's limitations will be our guide for recovery. Using the tools we have learned and our common sense will be our action. Most of us will not lose our fear overnight. Nor will we come to know our bodies capabilities and it's limitations overnight. This is a process. We will come to learn what we can do, what we can try, and what we know we must not do. But most important, we will come to know we can live our lives without the constant fear of re-injury. Do I allow the fear of re-injury to stop me from living?

Higher Power, please help me be aware of the possibilities of re-injury, but also the possibilities of living my life.

Higher Power, please help me cope with my pain today!

Life isn't always as serious as we make it out to be. There can be laughter in almost any situation, if we choose to seek it out. For those of us with chronic pain, we will come to find that laughter can be our best friend. For those who refuse to laugh, we say, lighten-up. Our injuries are sure to put us in some very compromising and embarrassing situations in our recovery and without the ability to laugh at ourselves we're in for some painful experiences. Do I find humor within myself and in the situations around me?

Higher Power, please help me realize that laughter can be a part of my life. Help me learn to laugh with others as well as with myself. Show me that laughter can help ease my pain and life's problems.

Higher Power, please help me cope with my pain today!

Today we're no longer bound for perfection. We're progress bound. We're entering a era and beginning a new direction. One that is measured by our daily progress rather than driven by perfection. A direction that we will see our results rather than striving for results we never see. We're moving towards accepting ourselves for what we have done rather than shaming ourselves for what is never good enough. We're going in a direction where mistakes can be free of guilt and full of opportunities for growth. For today, we are progress bound. Am I progress bound or am I still seeking perfection?

Higher Power, please help me strive for progress today, not perfection.

Higher Power, please help me cope with my pain today!

Many of us have tried giving up our pain killers, only to return. We have convinced ourselves that our emotional and physical pain was too much to tolerate without the drugs. But we should not be too quick to blame ourselves. Our past has shown us that our pain killers have worked, so we retreated to what we knew helped ease our pain.

Many have screamed out, "I can't. I've tried it before and I won't try again. I'm not living with this pain without my medication." We understand. We understand the fear and the dilemma you are feeling. We also know that pain killers, street drugs, and alcohol are not permanent solutions to our physical or emotional pain. The solution is to learn how to manage our physical and emotional pain, rather than masking it with chemicals. We believe that in the long run, we stand a better chance of managing our pain and coping with our life's situations if we are free of chemicals. Do I use pain killers for my emotional and physical pain today?

Higher Power, please help me cope with my pain without pain killers today. Help me accept that there are others who absolutely need their medication to live each day and that is between them and their Higher Power, not me.

Higher Power, please help me cope with my pain today!

Most days we are but characters who want to run the show and arrange everything to our liking. If the show is a flop we look to blame others instead of taking responsibility ourselves.

We can not control anyone or anything but ourselves today. Our lives are not based on being the director of a play and having people do as we say. Others have their own roles to play in life and no matter what type of directing we try to do, they will only fulfill their own roles.

We must remember that our Higher Power is in charge of running our show. We are in charge of ourselves only. Our Higher Power has a plan for each and every one of us. When we try to play the roles of the divine director we have taken our faith back and begun to run the show. Am I running the show today or am I letting my Higher Power direct my life?

Higher Power, please take away my need to run the whole show. Please grant me the faith to believe you know what is best for me and everyone else today.

Higher Power, please help me cope with my pain today!

129

Anyone of us, at any time, can come up with excuses why we shouldn't exercise. Especially if we have chronic pain. Some excuses may be valid, but for the most part, they are nothing more than excuses.

We tell ourselves we hurt and that any exercise will increase our pain. We have talked ourselves into believing that any form of exercise will lead to reinjury. We have convinced ourselves that we are embarrassed by our bodies and that no one can ever see us in this kind of condition. Some have come to the conclusion, what's the use. I haven't made any progress and exercising more, surely won't help matters.

Our excuses are sure to keep us from getting better, and in some cases, they may even assist in our physical deterioration. We are not asked to do it all today or to have a perfect exercise program. All we are asked is to begin putting our excuses aside and take that first step towards getting better. Do I make excuses about exercising today?

Higher Power, please help me trade my excuses for willingness and motivation.

Higher Power, please help me cope with my pain today!

MAY

Making a commitment to manage our pain has to come before any other and cannot be taken lightly. Our success will depend on our willingness and desire to make this commitment. Remember, God helps those who help themselves and we get out of it what we put in to it. Simple? Hardly. Our commitment will demand a great deal from us. Our patience will be tested and our egos challenged. We will want to take an easier softer way at times and some may even want to give up. But as we progress on our journey, we are certain to discover the benefits of our commitment to managing our pain have been worth all our efforts. Have I made my commitment today?

Higher Power, please grant me the strength and courage to make and carry out my commitment for today.

Higher Power, please help me cope with my pain today!

Summer is arriving and with it comes many changes. The trees bud, the flowers bloom and the sun shines bright. The smell of growth and hope fills the air. There are people biking, walking and filling the parks. It is a joyous time.

However, for some of us summer can be a discouraging and depressing time. We're not biking nor are we walking. We are at home in our darkness wishing our pain would disappear and that we could once again see greener grass. Do I smell the growth and hope in the air today or do I remain a prisoner of my pain?

Higher Power, please help me see the many changes that are possible for me today.

Higher Power, please help me cope with my pain today!

We have been conditioned to think that we can and must do it all. We have unwillingly been voted the almighty. We are the one's that must be the bread winners, take care of the family, hold a second job and be members of our community. We are the ones who must do it all.

But for many of us with chronic pain, life had to change. Our egos continued to think we were the almighty ones, but we were not. In fact we were quite different. We were no less of a person for this. Our lives were altered, that's all. Our condition had demanded we give up our role as the almighty one, put our ego's aside and become practical. Have I surrendered to a practical way of living or do I continue to struggle with my ego?

Higher Power, please quiet my ego in times of questioning. Please let me be practical and not the almighty one.

Higher Power, please help me cope with my pain today!

How many times have we said to ourselves, "this pain is driving me crazy, or others sure seem to treat me as if I were crazy, so I must be?" Relax, we're not going crazy. Chances are we're afraid and confused and we have every right to be. We've been thrust into a new way of living that has challenged our every thought and emotion. Our pain and our new situations has brought many of us to our knees to question the stability we once held so close.

For many of us with chronic pain, thinking these types of thoughts is quite normal. Where we begin our difficulties is when we begin acting on these thoughts. Thinking what we may consider is crazy is one thing. Acting out these thought is another. Today, it is our choice to think of these thoughts or we can act on them. Do I act on my crazy thoughts today?

Higher Power, please help me realize I don't need to act on every thought I have today.

Higher Power, please help me cope with my pain today!

At times we may say to ourselves, "I can move that, it doesn't look that heavy, what will they think of me if I don't move it? I'd better move it". This is our false pride playing games with us. When we allow our false pride to take over our better judgement, we have opened the door for disaster.

With our conditions we need to be fully aware of our false pride and conscious of our better judgement. Playing the bigshot or trying to be someone we're not will only hurt us. We have enough pain in our lives and we certainly do not need to invite more. Today we have a choice. We can listen to our false pride or we can listen to our better judgement. Do I use my false pride to feel better about myself?

Higher Power, please take away my false pride today and replace it with your better judgement.

Higher Power, please help me cope with my pain today!

Many of us who have chronic pain have spent many hours staring at blank walls. We ask ourselves why, why me? What did I do to deserve this? Did I do something wrong? Does God hate me? Of course not. We are victims of circumstance, we were in the wrong place at the wrong time or our bodies had said enough and they gave way.

Whatever our answers are, it's time we started working towards acceptance. By splashing and thrashing in the pool of victimization, the only result will be to drown in our self pity. Our hope for a new life is to escape that role of being a victim and begin to take our lives back. Am I a victim of chance today or am I a victim of my own self pitty?

Higher Power, please give me the courage to take my life back and to learn to accept that I am just a victim of chance.

Higher Power, please help me cope with my pain today!

The sun is out. We look out the window but we can't see it. Our mind is going a thousand miles and hour. Were thinking of yesterday and dreaming of tomorrow. Pain makes it's morning call and our mind shifts to it. We still don't know the sun is out.

The afternoon fades to darkness. We have thought about all our problems for the day but accomplished very little. The pain increases from the day's stress and our mind shifts back to it. We never knew the sun was out. We had missed it. The sun only rises and sets so many times for us, then it shines no longer. We cannot afford to miss one day of it's light. We cannot afford to be consumed by yesterday, tomorrow, or our pain. We must focus on today, for the sun is out. Am I living one day at a time?

Higher Power, please help be consumed only with today. Not yesterday or tomorrow or my pain.

Higher Power, please help me cope with my pain today!

Quiet time is a must for those of us with chronic pain. Our physical, psychological and our spiritual health depends upon it. Many of us have run our lives in excess before our injury and continue to today. We haven't given our bodies a break, a chance to rebuild themselves. We continue to demand more from them even though they do not give what they once used to.

We continue to overload ourselves psychologically. We think and process more than we really need to. We are preoccupied with yesterday and were plotting our futures. We have forgotten about what we have today. Spiritually, many of us have become bankrupt. But we have not forgotten about our Higher Power, we just haven't taken the time to acknowledge His or Hers presence. Do I take quiet time for myself and my Higher Power?

Higher Power, please help me realize how important my quiet time is for me today.

Higher Power, please help me cope with my pain today!

Many of us with chronic pain have been cast aside. Some have thought we were no longer good enough or capable of the task at hand. As a result, many of us have flirted with the prospect of our own death. We popped pills or used alcohol hoping our physical and emotional pain would go away. When it didn't, we had come to the conclusion we were no longer worth saving.

Some have acted on these thoughts and others have refused to accept this option. We thought we were worth saving. We knew our lives would one day turn around. Sanity would return to our lives. We would once again feel good about ourselves and learn new tasks within our restrictions. In spite of all that we had been through, we knew we were worth saving. Do I feel I'm worth saving or do I believe others opinions?

Higher Power, please let me know I am worth saving.

Higher Power, please help me cope with my pain today!

141

Some of us have stopped fighting and others have not. Some have accepted their new life, while others continue to search for their past. Some have accepted their pain is chronic in nature, while others search frantically for a cure. Some have surrendered and others continue to fight.

Whatever our case, our life's direction is sure to be influenced on whether we have stopped fighting or we continue to fight for that piece of control.

When we stop fighting with ourselves, our families, our employees, and with our pain, we are sure to discover that inner peace we have long searched for. We will no longer be at odds with ourselves or the world around us. We will have found our life's direction. Have I stopped fighting for the piece of control?

Higher Power, please help me accept my life for what it is today. Help me be at peace with myself and the world around me.

Higher Power, please help me cope with my pain today!

Some of us blame ourselves for our pain and for the position we're in. We tell ourselves, "if I had only moved out of the way, taken a different street or called in sick that day, none of this would have happened". Sure, hindsight is twenty-twenty, but it can't apply to us. We were injured and that's just the way it is.

None of us set out with the intentions of getting hurt. So why do we continue to blame ourselves? When we blame ourselves for what has happened chances are we will continue to feel guilty, ashamed, and angry. Our likelihood of getting better physically, emotionally and spiritually are nil. The key to healing ourselves will be patience, prayer, and acceptance. Without practicing these principles, we are certain to continue to blame ourselves. Do I blame myself for what has happened to me?

Higher Power, please help me stop blaming myself and help me learn to accept myself.

Higher Power, please help me cope with my pain today!

For a period of time we may have lost our purpose
in life. All we could see is that our life, as we knew it,
had been taken away and we were left with our pain.
We no longer belonged in the same circle of friends.
Our employer no longer wanted us. Our positions in
the community were soon filled by others. Our sense
of belonging had slowly slipped away.

As our recovery progresses, we may tend to be
impatient and grasp for a place to belong. That place
where we feel wanted and needed. A place where we
will be accepted as we are. That place where we can
share our love and our talents. That special place we
feel we belong.

We must practice patience. Our Higher Power
knows of such a place for us. When we are ready we
will be shown the way to our place where we belong.
Do I believe my Higher Power will guide me to the
place I belong?

Higher Power, please help me have patience and
faith that you will lead me to the place I belong.

Higher Power, please help me cope with my pain today!

It seems in today's world we're always wanting more. We're trying to keep up with the Joneses, and for what? It's all right to want to do better for ourselves and our families . But at what point do we say enough? When we get too busy wanting more, we tend to let our families and friends fall by the way side. We forget to take care of ourselves physically and emotionally and we become a wreck. All that we have accomplished has faded into the past without recognition. So we strive for even more.

As we frantically seek more for ourselves the price we pay rises as well. Our pain increases, our emotional and spiritually life decays, and we no longer comprehend the word serenity. But we continue to want more and we no longer accept what our Higher Power has given us today. Do I continue to want more?

Higher Power, please help me to accept what you have given me today. Help me use my better judgement in deciding how much more I really need.

Higher Power, please help me cope with my pain today!

Many of us with chronic pain have had financial difficulties. We were unable to go to work but the bills kept coming. This left us with financial fears and the uncertainty of our future. This however doesn't give us the right to avoid our responsibilities. If does however give us the right to shake off our financial fears.

When we continue to worry about what we have little control over, we are apt to drive ourselves to the edge of despair. By accepting our financial situation and our current ability to rectify it, we invite peace and serenity to overcome our fears and projections of the future. Can I shake off my financial fears?

Higher Power, please help me take responsibility for my finances today. Help me realize after I have done all I can it is time for acceptance and faith.

Higher Power, please help me cope with my pain today!

146

Faith is a belief. A feeling. A trust. A reliance on someone or something greater than ourselves. Many of us with chronic pain have at one time or another sought out the faith we had come to know. Some have sought this faith to help them cope with their pain, while others have sought direction and asked for peace.

Seeking faith today is our choice. It is not something we can demand to have in times of flair-ups or in time of immediate despair. It is not a convenient escape or a quick fix to any of our problems. It is a continual search from within and a continual commitment to grow towards our beliefs. Whatever type of faith we choose to believe in today, we must remember, it is ours and no one can take it from us, except ourselves. Am I seeking faith today?

Higher Power, help me accept the faith I have chosen today. Grant me the strength to maintain all that I believe each day.

Higher Power, please help me cope with my pain today!

For many of us our pain has become our enemy. All we had learned from it, is that it's constant and it has set out to destroy our lives. We never imagined for one moment that our pain in some indirect way, could help us make progress. However, when we surrender and let our pain become our teacher rather than our enemy, we are sure to begin making progress.

We must be open-minded and willing to explore the alternatives that are put in our path if we expect to make progress. If we remain timid and afraid of our pain, we are apt to learn very little or ever yet, remain as we are. Do I believe I can learn and make progress from my pain?

Higher Power, please take away the hate I have for my pain. Please help my pain become my teacher rather than my enemy.

Higher Power, please help me cope with my pain today!

We have all paid a tremendous price to get where we are so far. Chances are we will have to pay even more if we are to proceed. There are no free rides. No one will step forward and manage our pain for us or restore our emotional and spiritual health. These rides we must pay for ourselves.

However, there are some of us who refuse to pay their way and own their share of responsibility. We may think others owe us for what has happened, that it's their fault and they are the ones who should pay. Sorry. This is one ride they can't pay for. As the saying goes, "we can pay now or we can pay later". It is our choice. Do I expect a free ride or am I willing to work for what I need?

Higher Power, please help me accept that there are no free rides when it comes to my physical, emotional and spiritual wellness. It is I that must take responsibility.

Higher Power, please help me cope with my pain today!

For many of us there was a time or several times when we thought we couldn't live one more minute with our pain. Our once calm lives now seemed to be out of control. We cried out to our Higher Power for help and comfort. The next thing we knew, we had made it through a few more hours and a few more days. We had discovered that by putting our life in our Higher Power's hands, we gained a sense of calmness and direction. We no longer had to walk our journey alone. Have I put my life in my Higher Power's hands for today?

Higher Power, please take my life in your hands today. Please help me realize that together we can cope with whatever crosses our path.

Higher Power, please help me cope with my pain today!

I've heard others speak about me. I've heard them say I would never be the same as I once was. That I had gained a few pounds. That I was walking differently than before. That I had become depressed and I was withdrawn. That I no longer told my corny jokes. I heard them whispering about the medications I've taken and the funny braces I've worn. I've heard them call me a freeloader and a fraud. I've heard just about all of it. But I haven't heard many of them say, "I'm worth waiting for".

I haven't heard them say that I've been injured. That I'm trying to begin a new life. That I'm still a great person and a friend. I haven't heard many of them say, "we'll support you, we'll be patient just as you are". All I have really heard is what they haven't told me. Do I believe I'm worth waiting for today?

Higher Power, please help me realize that I am worth waiting for today.

Higher Power, please help me cope with my pain today!

Many of us have done things in the past that we are not proud of. Some have been before our injuries and others have been in spite of them. Whatever the case may be, it is time to make restitution to ourselves and to others. It is time we clear our conscience and take responsibility for our past actions.

But we must be patient. Many have not been able to even begin this process until they had a firm grasp on their pain problem. The honesty and willingness that this process requires will be difficult at best to muster until we have come to terms with our own situations first. Then we may begin taking care of our past and begin moving forward to our future. Have I begun cleaning up my actions from the past?

Higher Power, please grant me the honesty and the courage to take responsibility for my past actions. Help me strive to have a clear conscience today.

Higher Power, please help me cope with my pain today!

There comes a point for all of us when we're faced with just how serious our program of recovery is. This may come about from an emotional relapse, a flare-up or from reinjuring ourselves.

Whatever our reminder may be, now we must do something about it. Committing ourselves to managing our pain is a great place to start. Without it, we stand little chance at recovery. We must keep in mind we're talking about life and death for some of us.

It is up to us to decide how serious we want to be about our program today. No one can persuade us or do the work for us. We must decide the seriousness of our program. Am I serious about my recovery?

Higher Power, please help me realize that my attitude towards recovery today can be the difference between life and death tomorrow.

Higher Power, please help me cope with my pain today!

We will find in the process of managing our pain that many requests will be made of us. We won't like some of them and that's all right. But chances are we will need to comply with them anyway. Sometimes the things that are best for us are the hardest for us to do. All we need to do is ask ourselves, is what is being asked of me good for me? If the answer is yes, chances are we need to do it. We may not like it or fight and complain the whole way through, but our efforts are sure to be rewarded. Do I realize there are things that will be asked of me that I won't like but I will need to do them anyway?

Higher Power, please help me accept and carry out those things that I am asked to do even though I don't like them.

Higher Power, please help me cope with my pain today!

Many of us with chronic pain have sat idle for great lengths of time due to our injury and pain. As we begin our recovery process, we become excited at the possibilities that lie ahead. Our response is to make up for what we have lost. As a result, many of us neglect to finish all that we have started and we begin slipping backwards.

If we are to take full advantage of the possibilities in our recovery, we must begin by learning how to finish what we have started. We must learn to be patient and come to realize that all things can come to us in time. Do I finish things today?

Higher Power, please help me be patient today. Help me learn how to finish what I have started and to accept I no longer need to make up for lost time or for any possessions I may have lost.

Higher Power, please help me cope with my pain today!

In the midst of our pain we may have been less able to tolerate ourselves and others. Every other day our levels of tolerance seemed to change. Along the way we may have made an enemy or two. Whatever our case, we needed to change our attitudes towards tolerance.

If we want tolerance for our view point then we must also have tolerance for the view point of others. We don't have to like it or believe it, just strive to accept it. The same is true for ourselves. When our pain is intolerable, we must strive to accept ourselves and it's conditions. Lashing out at others or punishing ourselves will only make matters worse. Do I tolerate myself and others today?

Higher Power, Help me strive to be tolerant of myself and others today.

Higher Power, please help me cope with my pain today!

We have practiced many ways of managing our pain. We feel confident that we're doing a great job. However, we must not become complacent with our progress. We all have room for improvement and growth in managing our pain as well as in our daily affairs.

Continued improvement in these areas requires consistent practice in what we have learned. Without improvement we either stay the same, or worse, slip backwards, making it much harder to retain what we have achieved. Remember, improvement is achieved one day at a time. With practice, patience and prayer we are sure to make progress. Have I become complacent?

Higher Power, show me how I can improve myself today. Help me realize that becoming complacent will only hurt me not improve me.

Higher Power, please help me cope with my pain today!

When most of us hear the word exercise, our hair stands on end. We cry out, "No it hurts". This is not for me. Nonetheless, exercise is a key component of managing our pain. It's not a diet nor a supplement we can start and stop on a whim. We can't lose five pounds or gain ten pounds and quit. Exercise is our physical and emotional life line. Without exercising, we are sure to decay and slip back to our physical and emotional turmoil. For some, this will come quickly and for others, it may take some time, but we are all sure to end up in our own turmoil. Do I take my exercise program seriously today?

Higher Power, please help me realize how important exercise can be for me today.

Higher Power, please help me cope with my pain today!

Some of us have been inactive for long periods of time due to our injury. What energy we could muster was spent focused on the frustrations of our pain and on the fantasies of how we could put our lives back to the way they were. Eventually, we had run out of energy.

In the process of recovery, our goal is to begin refocusing our energy from our frustrations and our fantasies to hope and reality. To begin learning and using our energy for managing our pain and living our lives to their fullest.

We may come to find that our energy will run in cycles. Some have more energy in the morning, while others have more in the evening. We must learn to schedule our days according to our cycles. In time, most will come to find that we have more energy than we could have ever imagined having. Do I have a lack of energy today?

Higher Power, please help me realize it will take time to rebuild my energy level. Help me be patient enough today to do what I can with the energy I have.

Higher Power, please help me cope with my pain today!

The main goal of our recovery is to manage our pain. Without doing just that, we are certain to slip backwards. By now many of us are aware of that fact. What we may not be aware of, is the importance of practicing what we have learned in other aspects of our daily lives. Just as we are responsible for managing our pain, we must also be responsible for all other areas of our life.

Taking care of our personal matters and keeping ourselves fit physically, emotional, and spiritually are equally as important as managing our pain. These areas and others are part of our daily lives. By putting them into practice we are certain to move forward and reduce our chances of slipping backwards. Do I practice what I have learned?

Higher Power, please grant me the courage and strength to practice what I have learned in all my affairs.

Higher Power, please help me cope with my pain today!

Many of us have been harboring resentments from the beginning of our injury. Some feel they have been wronged by others and some resent how their lives have come about. Others have directly or indirectly held resentments towards themselves and their pain.

Our first reaction towards those we resent is retaliation. We feel we must get even and pay back others for what they have done to us. We have decided that there could have been no mistake made. Their intentions were to hurt us and they must be held responsible. But mostly, we resented ourselves. We had blamed ourselves for our injury and our pain, but all along we had directed our resentments towards others. Do I have resentments towards myself and others today?

Higher Power, please help me face my resentments today.

Higher Power, please help me cope with my pain today!

Gaining serenity means just that. Gaining it. Slowly, step by step, serenity can replace our once torn and uncomfortable thoughts. When we work towards spiritual progress, focus on changing the things we can change and letting go of the things we cannot change, serenity is certain to follow.

For some of us, serenity will come faster than it will for others. We all learn and accept things in our own way but we all seek the same results, serenity and peace of mind. Today we are granted the opportunity of working with our Higher Power and changing our attitudes about what we can and cannot change and what we choose to accept and not to accept. The result can be peace of mind and serenity for today. Am I gaining serenity and peace of mind in my life?

Higher Power, please help me gain serenity and peace of mind one step at a time and grant me the courage to do what is necessary to achieve them.

Higher Power, please help me cope with my pain today!

As time passes we may find ourselves slipping back into our old habits. Our once everyday prayer and meditation has become sporadic. Our exercise program has faded into our comfortable couch and remains just an idea. Working with others and attending support groups has slowly faded into selfishness. We have traded the very basics that removed us from our despair for laziness or some conveniences.

Today it is time we got back to the basics that have lifted us to the level of success we have achieved. A basic solid routine of prayer, meditation, exercise, attending support groups, and working with others. Without working these basic steps, we're sure to continue to fall backwards and eventually slip into the despair we started from. Have I slipped away from the basics of my recovery?

Higher Power, please help me get back to the basics of my recovery today.

Higher Power, please help me cope with my pain today!

JUNE

Some of us with chronic pain may have been accused or charged with free-loading, looking for a quick buck, or perhaps cheating some type of system we were once in. We must remember, just because the eyes and hearts of others may be filled with guilt, that doesn't mean we have to be included. We have enough of our own guilt and we certainly do not need more from others.

We did not set out one day to become injured or to have an extended vacation laying on our couch. Today, we are only guilty of having pain, nothing more. It is an unwanted change that we must grow to accept and learn to live with. Being guilty as charged is neither good nor bad. It's just the sentence that was given to us. Have I felt the guilt put upon me from others and myself?

Higher Power, please help me come to terms with any guilty feelings I may have today.

Higher Power, please help me cope with my pain today!

Many of us came to the conclusion that we were no longer worth much to ourselves or to anyone else. We had decided our injury had turned us into something others may refer to as junk. We decided that we belonged with all the other junk that doesn't perform up to the standards of ourselves and others.

But we may have been too hasty in our decision. God doesn't make junk. We are the ones who take it upon ourselves to declare ourselves useless and worthless. We have yet to see what we are capable of and the goodness that lies within. Do I know God doesn't make junk?

Higher Power, please help me accept myself with my imperfections today.

Higher Power, please help me cope with my pain today!

After our injuries, many of us have come to realize that our sex lives were no longer what they used to be. Some had lost all desire for closeness and others felt inadequate about the whole situation. What balance and passion we once had with ourselves and our partner had vanished.

We must not get too discouraged. There is hope for us. Many people who have chronic pain have worked through their situation and regained a sense of balance with themselves and others. We must be willing to take that first step and put our pride and embarrassment aside and be honest with ourselves and others. As a result of this, we can go on working our way towards a new balance. Am I comfortable with my sexuality today?

Higher Power, please help me put my pride and embarrassment aside and take that first step towards regaining my balance.

Higher Power, please help me cope with my pain today!

Many of us with chronic pain had become familiar with expecting the worst of things to happen in our lives. We had parts of our lives taken away piece by piece only to be replaced by shattered hopes and expectations. As the days went on, we had lost all hope and we no longer expected the worst, we were sure it would happen.

We had lost our positive attitude and outlook on life. We had grown an extra set of eyes in the back of our heads. We expected the worst from all sides and that's just what happened. When we continually look and expect the worst to happen, chances are that's what will happen. We must keep in mind, none of us are jinxed or cursed. We have chronic pain and good things can come our way if we let them. Do I expect the worst to always happen or have I begun looking for the good in my life?

Higher Power, please help me keep a positive attitude and out-look today. Help me learn to look for good and not the worst.

Higher Power, please help me cope with my pain today!

With chronic pain we inevitably will have flare-ups and set-backs. Some may have several and others just a few. But we all have a choice on how we let them affect us. We can let our flare-ups and set-backs take over our lives for days, for weeks, or even for months, or we can begin to work through them and use them as opportunities to grow. This is our time to learn just what causes our flair-ups and what events led us to our set-backs. It's a time to use new techniques and a time to reach out to others and use the support around us. The more successful we are today at working through our flair-ups and set-backs, the less our pain can control our lives and hold us prisoners as it once did. Do I use my flair-ups and set-backs as opportunities to grow or do I use them as excuses to feel sorry for myself?

Higher Power, please help me accept that flair-ups and set-backs are a part of having chronic pain. Please help me use them as opportunities to grow and move forward rather than as excesses to move backwards.

Higher Power, please help me cope with my pain today!

In the beginning of our recovery, many of us realized we were having little fun. Some had plain forgotten how and others were so afraid of their pain they wouldn't allow themselves the opportunity.

Having chronic pain does not mean we are sentenced to a life of boredom and unhappiness. It does mean, if we are to have fun in our recovery, it is our responsibility to seek it out. The days of expecting others to make us happy are gone.

Today is our day to cast our fears aside and begin having fun. Do I have fun in my recovery?

Higher Power, please help me put my fears aside so I may begin experiencing the joy of recovery.

Higher Power, please help me cope with my pain today!

Many of us with chronic pain have felt trapped at one time or another and felt there was nowhere to go. We asked, "where do I go for relief, who do I tell about my crazy thoughts, and where do I go with my life?" Many of us had no answers and the ones that were suggested by others, we certainly didn't care for. So where do we go?

It has been suggested we get on our knees and ask our Higher Power for the guidance we have been lacking. When our will has failed and others cannot help, there is but one other direction we need to go. To our Higher Power. Do I feel there is nowhere to go or anybody I can turn to today?

Higher Power, when I feel trapped and that I have nowhere to go, please reassure me I can come to you.

Higher Power, please help me cope with my pain today!

Those of us with chronic pain have plenty of reasons to be angry. With little effort, most of us could come up with a long list of things that angered us and most likely, we could add something new to it each day. However, there are consequences of this unresolved anger.

We are at risk of becoming a bitter, spiteful, and rageful person. We can eventually develop serious resentments and bring about depression. Our pain increases and our mental, physical, and spiritual condition suffers greatly. Our unresolved anger had taken control of us just as our pain once did.

Learning to cope with our anger will not be an overnight task. At times it can be a frustrating and confusing process. But with prayer, practice, patience, and persistence, we can learn to cope with our anger. Do I cope with my anger appropriately today?

Higher Power, help me resolve any issues I may have with anger today.

Higher Power, please help me cope with my pain today!

Before we learned how to walk we had to learn to crawl and then stand. This process for most was a slow turn of events.

Learning to live a life with chronic pain is no different. It's slow turning but it does come about. Our frustrations and impatience are sure to show many times over. We will fall down over and over. Sometimes we will want to get up and try again and other times we won't. But by having faith and putting one foot in front of the other, our new lives will come about. Have I accepted that learning to live my life with chronic pain will take time and patience?

Higher Power, please give me the courage to learn how to live with my pain. Please help me accept that this process may take time, but eventually it can come about.

Higher Power, please help me cope with my pain today!

When it comes to chronic pain we cannot afford to kid ourselves. This is serious business. We can't afford to kid ourselves about how much pain we're in or not in, or about what we're able or not able to do, or about how good or bad something may be in our lives.

Kidding ourselves can be dangerous physically and emotionally. It has the potential to set us back to the despair we had come from, or possibly led us to places where we are sure to experience more pain than is necessary.

As our recovery progresses, so must our level of honesty. This level of self-honesty may not come easy for some. Remember, we are admitting to our faults and to those things many of us have been trying to avoid for some time. All we are asked to do today, is to be willing to be honest with ourselves and eventually, we will no longer wish to kid ourselves. Am I kidding myself today or do I search for the truth?

Higher Power, please help me to not kid myself today. Help me learn to search out the truth about myself.

Higher Power, please help me cope with my pain today!

Seeing the beauty in life hasn't come easy for some of us with chronic pain. Our lives had become a pattern of shattered dreams and faded hopes. Our hearts and eyes had begun feeling and seeing nothing but pain. Somehow we had lost track of the beauty that lies within ourselves.

For some, that was our past and for others, it is our present. Learning to see the beauty in our lives begins with reshaping our attitude and beginning to feel grateful for what is around us. At first we may have a difficult time of this and become discouraged. Our old attitudes may want us to believe that all is wrong and all is ugly. But as we progress in our recovery, we are sure to begin seeing the beauty in our lives. Have I discovered the beauty in my life or do I look for what is painful and ugly?

Higher Power, please help me strive daily to seek the beauty in my life. Help me grow to accept and learn from all that may be painful and ugly.

Higher Power, please help me cope with my pain today!

The most common and deadly defects for those who have chronic pain are workaholic tendencies, perfectionism, unresolved anger, and co-dependency. These defects, when taken to the extreme, can halt our progress and eventually lead us back to that pain and despair we once knew so well.

Dealing with these and other defects we may have today, will be partly our responsibility. Recognizing these defects when they appear will be our first step. The second step will be asking our Higher Power to help take them away from us. The third step requires that we be persistent and patient. We didn't develop these defects overnight and we certainly won't be cleansed of them overnight. Do I have deadly defects today?

Higher Power, help me realize that I too share the responsibility for having my defects removed. Help me be persistent and patient as we do our work.

Higher Power, please help me cope with my pain today!

When we found out our pain wasn't going to go away, we may have thought our lives were over, or that we had reached a dead end.

Many of us may feel this way, but there is a life to enjoy for those of us who have chronic pain. Life doesn't have to be a dead-end. We have the opportunity to live our lives to the fullest each day. We can make our journey as long as we would like it to be or we can create our own dead end. Today, the choice is ours. Do I believe my life is a dead end or do I create my own opportunities?

Higher Power, please help me realize that life with chronic pain doesn't have to be a dead end. Rather it can be a new beginning.

Higher Power, please help me cope with my pain today!

The obstacles we face in our everyday life and those that accompany chronic pain, can at times seem overwhelming. When this happens, we need only look back at what we went through to reach this point in our recovery. We will come to see that our Higher Power never puts more than we can handle in front of us at any one time.

Many of us will come to know that our Higher Power has given us the courage and strength to overcome these obstacles. But now it is time that we learn to use what has been given to us and begin to move forward. Do I feel I can overcome any obstacles that are put in my path today?

Higher Power, please help me understand that obstacles are put in my path to learn and grow from and to overcome. Help me realize that together we can overcome any obstacle that is put in our path.

Higher Power, please help me cope with my pain today!

The key to willingness for many is just that, to be willing. In the beginning of our recovery, the smallest attempt to put the key in the door of willingness is all that is needed. Once the key has been turned, we can always open the door a little at a time.

Many of us may find that our self-will will want to slam the door shut from time to time. We will want to regress back to our old comfortable ways and try to take control of the situation. We must not be too hard on ourselves. All we are asked to do is to become willing. That's all. Have I begun opening the door to willingness today?

Higher Power, please give me the faith and courage to become willing. Help me realize that there are many new opportunities waiting for me beyond the doors of willingness.

Higher Power, please help me cope with my pain today!

When our pain finally won over us, our lives slowly began to vanish. We spent countless hours focusing on our pain and feeling sorry for ourselves and for what was happening to us. Day by day our lives were wasting away.

As we begin to get a hold on our pain, we will come to realize we do have a choice. We can continue to waste our lives away or we can begin living them. We can begin to be grateful for what we do have, rather than feeling sorry for ourselves for what we think we are missing.

Each day that we spend trapped and held prisoner by our pain, is one more day that has vanished and never to return. Am I wasting my life away today or am I living my life?

Higher Power, please help me take my life back today. Show me that my life is too valuable to waste away.

Higher Power, please help me cope with my pain today!

For those of us with chronic pain, learning to trust ourselves hasn't come easy. All we had listened to for sometime was our pain and fear. We had lost touch with that part of us that was trusting and made sense of all within and of the world around us.

Learning to trust ourselves again will require us to search out that part of us that has trusted in the past. To begin listening to ourselves and to take risks, rather than letting our fear and pain overrule the trust that is within. Do I have trust in myself today?

Higher Power, please help me learn how to trust myself today. Help me listen to that part of me that can trust and make sense of all around me.

Higher Power, please help me cope with my pain today!

Many of us have issues we have yet to resolve. Some have started the day we were introduced to our pain and others have had issues dating several years back.

Whatever our case, it is time to clean house. When we continue to live in our past or present issues, our pain will continue to grow as well. They are inseparable and will continue to follow us until each issue has been properly dealt with. Remember, each issue will have it's own set of circumstances and it's own time to dealt with. We must practice patience yet be persistent on our course to resolving our issues. Have I begun resolving my issues today?

Higher Power, please grant me the courage to begin resolving my issues today.

Higher Power, please help me cope with my pain today!

When we begin climbing out of a bout with depression, we must avoid trying to get our whole life back in order all at once. Taking on tasks that are too much for us or ones we are not ready for, will only set us up for failure and possibly push us back into our depression.

An attitude of all or nothing here can be most destructive. For our best chances of success, we must look at our situation as realistically as possible and proceed with a sense of caution. We must learn to be patient and begin climbing out of our depression one step at a time. We must also realize there are others who are willing to help. It is up to us to extend our hand and ask for the help and support we need. Do I ask for help when I have a bout with depression or do I try to do it all my way?

Higher Power, please grant me the courage and guidance I need to climb out of my depression whenever it becomes active.

Higher Power, please help me cope with my pain today!

When our pain had us defeated and we felt complete despair, we thought we were the only ones who could have felt the way we did. We felt entirely alone and that this was the way it was always going to be. We swore we felt loneliness like no others had.

For some of us, this loneliness would go away. We would renew our old friendships and make new ones. But others weren't as fortunate. They would continue to feel alone and desperate. All they had really wanted was someone who would care and understand. They wanted their loneliness to go away. If we are to rid ourselves of loneliness today, we must be willing to reach out to others and extend our hand and open our hearts. When this happens, we are on our way to ridding ourselves of loneliness. Do I feel lonely today?

Higher Power, please help me to reach out to others today. Help me not to feel alone and desperate and consumed with my pain.

Higher Power, please help me cope with my pain today!

When we are consumed and controlled by our pain changing our thoughts and actions seem almost impossible. We were no longer open to new ideas and our options had faded. We had become prisoners not only of our pain but of our ability to change.

Many of us began to realize that if we were to survive, we must somehow learn to change our attitude and outlook on life. Some of us prayed for courage and some prayed for the strength to survive until change for them was possible. Others had lost all hope and were certain the change they desperately wanted would never occur. They would remain prisoners of their pain and their ability to change. Have I given up on change in my life?

Higher Power, please grant me the ability to make whatever changes are necessary in my life today.

Higher Power, please help me cope with my pain today!

Many of us are still running scared from our pain. We haven't accepted the idea of living with our pain or it's limitations. We run and keep on running, hoping we can out run our pain, but we cannot. We can only run so far and hide so long until we are forced to come face to face with are pain and who and what we are.

Sometimes, what we are most afraid of isn't as terrible as we make it out to be. But we won't truly know that unless we stop running and begin to face our pain and fears. Have I decided to stop running and face my pain?

Higher Power, please help me face my pain and limitations today.

Higher Power, please help me cope with my pain today!

Some of us have said at one time or another that we were sure we would never be able to live with our pain. Yet today we are effectively managing our pain. For this to have happened, we had to take a risk. We had to move from our old comfortable way of doing things and try something different. We had no idea and no guarantees that this new way would work, yet we took that risk and sought another way of managing our pain.

Many of us are afraid to take risks because we're afraid of the unknown. When we take a risk, it's just that, a risk. We don't know what the outcome will be. The same is true when it comes to coping with our pain. We're not sure what will give us relief and what won't. But one thing we do know, if we don't begin taking risks today, we are sure to stay the same or slip backwards. Have I taken the risks necessary to manage my pain today?

Higher Power, please grant me the courage and faith to take a risk today.

Higher Power, please help me cope with my pain today!

Sometimes we are so consumed with the outcome of events that we overlook the possibility that there may be a lesson to be learned in the process. When we are having a flair-up, chances are we are worried only about reducing our pain and not learning any lessons. Nor are most of us looking to learn a lesson when we're in financial distress. We just want money.

We must remember, wisdom is not gained so much by the outcome of events. Rather it is gained by going through the process and the lessons we had learned along the way. As our recovery progresses there will be many lessons to be learned. We will have opportunities to learn about ourselves and about our pain. It will be up to us to choose if we are to focus only on the outcome of events, or we will be open minded and learn the lessons that are offered for us. Do I look for the lessons to be learned in my daily living, or do I focus on the outcome?

Higher Power, please help me become open minded today. Help me realize that the wisdom learned is sometimes far more valuable than the outcome of my efforts.

Higher Power, please help me cope with my pain today!

Part of living one day at a time is getting into the habit of taking a personal inventory. We ask ourselves if we had a good day. Did we stray away from our Higher Power? Did we harm anyone throughout the day? Have we lived each and every moment as if it may be our last or have we had one foot in yesterday and one in tomorrow? Have we accomplished what we had set out to for the day? Have we given of ourselves today or were we consumed with self-importance and attending to only our wants?

Learning to take a personal inventory and to live just for today many seem overwhelming at first, but it is possible to do. By reviewing our day we are able to keep a close check on our behaviors, on our attitudes, and on our daily progress. For all any of us really have, is today. Do I live just for today?

Higher Power, please teach me how to live just for today.

Higher Power, please help me cope with my pain today!

Living with chronic pain can be serious business. Yet as time passes and our lives become comfortable, many of us forget the seriousness of it all. We have forgotten the unhappiness and the uncertainty our pain had once caused us. Some have effortlessly cast aside the pain they had caused themselves and others. While some have forgotten the daily struggles we had endured just to function from one minute to the next.

When we have forgotten where we have come from and the seriousness of chronic pain, we have fallen off the path of recovery. We have begun slipping back to that place we worked so diligently to escape from. But today is a new day. A day for renewed commitment towards the seriousness of our recovery. To remember where we have come from and to remember what we need to do for our future. For today, this is the seriousness of it all. Do I take my recovery seriously or have I fallen victim to complacency?

Higher Power, please help me not to forget my past nor lose sight of what I must do for my future.

Higher Power, please help me cope with my pain today!

Some of us have had a difficult time of being honest with ourselves when it came to our pain and the damage it may have caused. We may tell ourselves our pain isn't as serious as it really is or that it hasn't changed any part of our life and it certainly hasn't affected our families or others around us. We know this is not so. Yet many of us have tried denying this for sometime.

Becoming honest with ourselves can be a difficult task. We are asked to look within ourselves and at the world around us and see things for what they really are, not for what we want them to be or think they should be. Being honest with ourselves is a black and white concept. We're either honest or we're not. We must be patient with ourselves as we begin learning our new ways. Many of us have never been faced with or have been asked to accept what we have been through. All many of knew was, if we denied what was happening, there was a chance it would just go away. Have I been willing to be honest with myself today?

Higher Power, please give me the courage and strength to be honest with myself today.

Higher Power, please help me cope with my pain today!

193

Many of us had lived alone with our pain for quite some time. We thought we were the only ones who had felt the way we did. When we found others who were like us, there was a sense of relief. We found we could share the things that others did not understand. We had found a sense of unity. A peace where we were all equal. We had found that special place where others would help us learn to manage our pain. What we had found was a support group for those who have chronic pain. Do I use a support group to help me manage my pain?

Higher Power, please help me realize that I no longer have to live alone with my pain. Show me there are others just like me who are willing to share their experiences, strengths, and hopes with me.

Higher Power, please help me cope with my pain today!

Some of us have said, "What ? Pleasure with pain? You've got to be kidding". Past experience has shown that once we started managing our pain and not letting our pain manage us, we begin to live life more fully. Living life can have it's many pleasures, even with chronic pain.

For some, this may be a hard concept to grasp at first, but it is possible. As we begin to let go of our pain and start focusing on the things that bring us pleasure, we have begun our journey towards finding pleasure with pain. Do I believe I can find the pleasure in my life despite my pain?

Higher Power, please help me realize that others are experiencing pleasure, even with their pain, and I can do the same.

Higher Power, please help me cope with my pain today!

Many of us had come to a point where all we wanted was to be left alone with our pain. Our attitudes and personality had reached a point where we began driving our families and friends further and further away from us. None of us really knew what to do, so we did nothing. As time passed, our family and friends were afraid to approach us. We were like time bombs waiting to explode.

Today we no longer have to avoid our family and friends. Nor do they need to avoid us. We've found a better way. We can begin sharing with one another. We can share our experiences, our feelings, our hopes and fears, and what we need from them to help support us. But we must be willing to take the first step and continue to reach out. Have I begun making peace with my relationships?

Higher Power, please help me realize how important my relationships are to me today. Help me take that first step and reach out to them.

Higher Power, please help me cope with my pain today!

JULY

It's a new day with old pain, but it doesn't seem to affect me as it once did. This morning I feel comfortable with myself and the world around me. I feel closer to my Higher Power than I did yesterday. I suddenly realize that it is a good morning. I was told my life would improve with time and patience. Maybe they were right.

It seems all I can remember about past mornings was my struggles and pain and how I would fill my days. Would anything change? Would today be the day I break free or would I remain a prisoner of my pain. Have my mornings improved?

Higher Power, please help me accept that not every morning will be as I would like it to be. But with patience, my good mornings can become abundant.

Higher Power, please help me cope with my pain today!

199

The effects of our pain go much deeper than we tend to believe. Our pain can affect our immediate families, our extended families, our friends and most people we may come in contact with. In most cases, when we're experiencing physical pain, those around us are experiencing emotional pain. They have at one time or another watched us crawl across the floor in pain or listened to us cry out for help, and in some cases, stood by helplessly as we had tried to take our own lives.

Today we can no longer afford to be selfish. Nor can we continue to exclude the feelings of those around us. Time and time again our pain knowingly or unknowingly has affected the very ones we love and who love us. We must begin in one shape or form to include those around us in our recovery. For today, chronic pain is a family affair. Do I realize chronic pain is a family affair?

Higher Power, please help me realize how my pain has affected others.

Higher Power, please help me cope with my pain today!

When we set forth to accomplish our tasks, we are usually guided by some form of expectation. In many cases, our expectations far exceed our capabilities. Consequently, the outcome of our work may be far less gratifying than we had anticipated.

Our expectations become harmful only when they are unrealistic or when we fail to accept their outcome. Keeping this in mind and the work that lies ahead in our recovery, many of us with chronic pain must re-evaluate our expectations. Our capabilities may not be what they used to be but our expectations remain the same. There are those who want to make up for what they feel they have lost or compensate for their injury. As a result, their expectations far exceed their capabilities and they become discouraged and even give up. Do I have unrealistic expectations of myself today?

Higher Power, please help me realize what I am capable of accomplishing today and help me see when my expectations are unrealistic.

Higher Power, please help me cope with my pain today!

We are not expected to make the transition from our previous life to a life with pain overnight. Nor are we expected to accept it overnight. We all accept and adapt to new situations in our own way and in our own time.

Most of us are sure to have moments when we will fight this acceptance tooth and nail. At times we may think that the acceptance will never come, but we must believe that with patience and prayer, it will. We must also believe that once we have accepted our new life, the opportunities for growth and improvement will grow in numbers. Our once confusing and orderless lives will again have direction. Have I accepted my new life?

Higher Power, please grant me the patience to accept my new life today.

Higher Power, please help me cope with my pain today!

Many of us have had our lives thrust ahead into a new time. We're in a new place with new pain and new directions. We have suddenly lost our once comfortable and meaningful lives. In a fraction of a second, time for us has been turned ahead to a place we never knew existed. A place with pain, with limitations, with difficult choices, and unexplored emotions.

For some, their time would stop with their injury. For others their time would move ahead. Some would waste their time as if it were plentiful, while others would cling to every moment. Some would grow to accept this time as theirs, while others have lost all hope for today and the time ahead. Have I accepted that today is the only twenty-four hours I really have?

Higher Power, please help me accept that I cannot go back in time or ahead and change my life as I would like it. All I have is today and all I can change is myself.

Higher Power, please help me cope with my pain today!

Most of us are grateful for our new beginning. A new life. An opportunity for new directions and new dreams. A chance to explore who we really are and what we have to offer others. A life filled with spirituality and void of hate and despair. A life that many of us have paid for with our hearts and souls.

Our new life has come to us with the highest price imaginable. Our pain. But when we realize where we have come from and where our despair may have led us, our pain is but a small price to pay for our new life. Am I grateful for my new life?

Higher Power, please help me accept my new life today.

Higher Power, please help me cope with my pain today!

Many have been consumed by their pain and it's symptoms for quite some time. We had lost all freedom to choose where we wanted to go with our lives. Our pain was directing our every thought and action. We had become powerless. For some of us, that was our past. For others, it has become the present.

Regaining our freedom to make choices and deciding where we want to go with our lives begins with learning how to manage our pain. We're clearly powerless and short on options when our pain holds us prisoners. As we begin to break free, our powerlessness is sure to fade and our options will become clearer. In time, this will give us a chance to decide where we want to go with our lives. Have I decided where it is I want to go?

Higher Power, please help me realize that to have choices in my life, I must first learn how to manage my pain.

Higher Power, please help me cope with my pain today!

Once we have been lifted from our depths of despair and we are no longer prisoners of our pain, our lives are certain to change and never be the same again.

We will have opportunities to achieve things we thought were impossible for us with the pain that we have. We will come to know and accept ourselves as we are and not for who we think we should become. We will know serenity and become at peace with the world around us. We will find the courage and the strength to cope with each day we face. Our feelings of hopelessness will be replaced with hope and faith. We will come to know that we are no longer alone and that there are others who are willing to help us. We will come to know our lives can change if we let them. Do I believe my life can change?

Higher Power, please help me realize that change in my life is possible and these things can materialize if I let them.

Higher Power, please help me cope with my pain today!

When we first begin managing our pain, we do it with a sense of immaturity. Some of us thought we had all the answers and our way was the only way. Others were just young and hadn't realized the magnitude of what was being asked of them. Whatever the case, we had some growing to do before we reached a level of maturity.

Part of reaching a level of maturity for those of us with chronic pain, means we have come to accept our situation and our new limitations. We will come to a point where we no longer have all the answers, but rather we have become teachable and willing to explore new ways of managing our pain and our lives.

As we progress along our new journey, our level of maturity may fall short of our expectations and ideals. But we must keep in mind, a sign of maturity is regaining our composure and moving forward. Have I matured when dealing with my pain?

Higher Power, please help me realize that it takes time to gain maturity. Help me be patient and open to new ways of living today.

Higher Power, please help me cope with my pain today!

How many times have you heard, "I don't know what's causing your pain but have you seen a psychiatrist?" That's what some of us with chronic pain have experienced.

We began to question ourselves. We ask, "Am I crazy? Is my pain all in my head?" Hardly. Our pain is real. We sleep with it, eat with it, and play with it.

We have been to the depths of our despair and back again with our pain. We may be confused and somewhat disoriented at times, but we're not crazy. Do I feel my sanity slipping away because of what others may be saying or do I believe my pain is real?

Higher Power, please reassure me that I am not losing my sanity today. Help me realize what is important is how I feel about myself and what I know about my pain.

Higher Power, please help me cope with my pain today!

208

Just because we have developed chronic pain doesn't mean we have to lose our sense of self. We continue to own our value system, our spiritual beliefs, and most of all our feelings, which is our very foundation. From these we can build a new sense of self.

When chronic pain entered our lives a new sense of self followed and for some of us it may have been negative. Our self-esteem may have been shattered. Our image of how we looked may have changed for the worse. However we may perceive ourselves today, we have an opportunity to develop a new sense of self. We can keep what we like about ourselves and strive to obtain what we would like to improve. One day we will have a new sense of self that we are comfortable with and love. Am I working toward developing a new sense of self?

Higher Power, please help me realize that I can develop a new sense of self that one day I will come to love and accept.

Higher Power, please help me cope with my pain today!

For some of us with chronic pain, we develop something called the trotters pace. We're not too fast and we're not too slow. We set our own pace according to our abilities and according to how we feel that day. We're not competing with others who may be faster. We just set our pace and do our best.

There will be others who will want to run to keep up with others or who refuse to set their pace. If they are capable of it, let them go ahead. Remember, our mission is to do our best, not to impress others. Have I accepted I must set my own pace and not compete with others?

Higher Power, please help me find my own pace today. Help me realize I need only impress myself today, not others.

Higher Power, please help me cope with my pain today!

Chronic pain not only affects us, it affects our family and friends as well. They have felt our pain and witnessed our descending journey to the depths of our despair. They have felt our frustration and our fear and they have come to know a pain all their own.

Today we must realize that our family and friends may need help just as we do. For one of us to get help and not the other can prove to be unsuccessful. In a relationship we look to each other for support and guidance, not for turmoil and frustration. To increase the chances of recovery within the family today, we must treat chronic pain as a family affair. Do I believe chronic pain had affected my family and friends?

Higher Power, please help me see that my pain has affected my family and friends. Grant us the courage to seek the support we need today.

Higher Power, please help me cope with my pain today!

When dealing with chronic pain some tough questions arise. For every tough question there is usually a tough answer. Chances are, we have been avoiding or unwilling to hear some of these answers for some time. Many of us have been avoiding our reality, while others have been unwilling to even ask these questions, let alone accept the answers.

We must keep in mind that chronic pain can be a life and death situation. We must learn to ask whatever it is we want to know and then listen for our answers. It may not always be what we want to hear or what we think is the right time for suggestions or caring advice. However, the answers we receive will probably be the best solutions to our problems. When we proceed with a closed mind and we are consumed with fear, we only delay the inevitable solutions we seek. Do I ask tough questions and expect simple answers, or am I willing to listen to all the answers that are given to me?

Higher Power, please help me learn how to ask for what I need today and to listen attentively for what it is I need to hear.

Higher Power, please help me cope with my pain today!

212

Whatever we tell ourselves, we are sure to become. If we tell ourselves we are worthless because of our injury, then that is what we will be. If we tell ourselves no one will love us because we have pain, we surely won't allow others to love us. If we tell ourselves our lives are over and we will never be successful again, then that is sure to be our destiny.

Many of us are faced with the fact that our bodies are no longer what they used to be and we are constantly reminding ourselves of this. Unfortunately, it is in a negative way. When we continually bombard ourselves with our negative thoughts, we have left no room for healing and we have felt no room for the healing talk that lies within. How do I talk to myself today?

Higher Power, please replace my negative talk with those thoughts that will begin to heal me today.

Higher Power, please help me cope with my pain today!

213

We look but we cannot see. We wonder why we have so much pain when we cannot see it's cause. Others may have said we look great, but we feel our pain. Some of us have become subjects of speculation and our honor has been questioned because others cannot see our pain. We suddenly realize we are no longer coping with our pain, rather we are defending it. Do I defend my pain today or do I manage it?

Higher Power, please help me learn to understand and manage my pain today. Help me have patience and understanding for those around me who cannot see or feel my pain.

Higher Power, please help me cope with my pain today!

When chronic pain has entered our home, chances it will never be the same again. It may have changed for the better or in some cases, for the worse. Some have altered their family roles and are doing quite well, while others remain in complete confusion about what roles each member should have. Some have learned to be constructive with the time they may have at home, while others pace the floor and bring about nervousness with other family members. Some have learned how to communicate their wants and needs with each member of the family, while others have remained demanding and aggressive. Whatever our case may be, there is no escaping the fact that chronic pain has entered our home. Have I accepted that chronic pain and all that accompanies it has entered my home?

Higher Power, please help me come to accept that my pain and all that accompanies it has entered my home. Help me realize that it is now partly my responsibility to cope with it.

Higher Power, please help me cope with my pain today!

Our program says to take life one day at a time and that's how we intend to do it. But what about tomorrow? Do we look forward to it? Do we have plans for tomorrow? Do our dreams include tomorrow, or do we even care about tomorrow?

It is said that if we stop caring about tomorrow, we may stop caring altogether and tomorrow turns into a string of endless days. Do I care about tomorrow or have I let tomorrow turn into a string of endless days that I care little about?

Higher Power, please stop tomorrow from becoming a string of days that never come. Please help keep my hopes and dreams alive so I may look forward to tomorrow.

Higher Power, please help me cope with my pain today!

We have gone to great lengths and put forth our best efforts to reach this point in our recovery. Our efforts to manage our pain have begun to pay off. We feel better than we have in quite some time. Yet we ask ourselves, "How much more? How long do I need to keep putting forth this kind of effort?"

There are no simple answers. However, we do know living with chronic pain demands our serious attention and effort if we are to make progress and manage our pain. We also know, all that is asked of us is to put forth our best effort. From our best efforts we are sure to experience the best results. Am I putting forth my best efforts today?

Higher Power, please help me put forth my best efforts today. Help me accept all that is required of me is to do my best.

Higher Power, please help me cope with my pain today!

My pain has faded time and time again but it has always returned. It won't go away, for I have asked it to several times. It may go away for a minute, an hour, or even a week but it always returns. Nobody really knows why my pain comes and goes.

Some have said, we would take it away if we knew how. But for today, it is your pain. You will have the opportunity to become friends with it, accept it and learn how to cope with it one day at a time. For this will be your key to peace and serenity. Your pain will fade from time to time, but the past has proven it will always return. Have I accepted my pain may fade from time to time but it is sure to return?

Higher Power, please help me accept that I have chronic pain and it may fade from time to time, but it will most likely continue to return.

Higher Power, please help me cope with my pain today!

Some of us have been managing our pain for months and even years. Along the way, we have learned through trial and error and from those who have much wisdom and experience. But there are others who are just beginning. The newcomer. The ones who have little or no experience at managing their pain.

These are the ones who will seek our help. They will want to know what we have learned. What has worked and what has not. They will come to us thirsty for knowledge. Our obligation is to share what we have learned. To help them as we were helped so they may one day help others and continue to do as experience does. Do I seek out others' experience and wisdom or do I pretend to know it all?

Higher Power, please help me reach out so I may gain the knowledge of others and to share what I have learned.

Higher Power, please help me cope with my pain today!

For some of us, our pain was brought on by some sort of traumatic event. One day we were pain free, the next day our lives were to be changed forever. When our recovery process started, we expected the same type of break-through or sudden event that would change us forever. We expected something quick and easy that would put us back on course.

As time passed we discovered there was no burning bush to guide us back on course or take away our pain. Rather, we discovered that this was to be a slow process, with many subtle signs to follow that would guide us and become our burning bush. Do I expect my life to change instantly, or do I believe my life will change and grow in time?

Higher Power, please help me realize that your guidance comes in many forms, not always through a burning bush of revelations.

Higher Power, please help me cope with my pain today!

When we enter recovery, we usually have high expectations of ourselves and others. Consequently, our expectations become barriers rather than motivaters. Some of us expect everything and we expect it to happen today. While others expect their lives will return to the way they were before their injury.

These are unrealistic expectations. All we have done is created a platform to fall from and barriers that have put limits on our progress.

When we have expectations of ourselves and others today, we must ask if they are realistic or unrealistic. Can I accept the results or will I continue to demand more? Whatever our answer, it will become our barriers to progress or our motivation to move ahead. Do I have unrealistic expectations of myself and others?

Higher Power, please help me find a balance with my expectations today.

Higher Power, please help me cope with my pain today!

Many of us have said, "I really feel stupid. If I hadn't been doing what I was doing, I wouldn't have been injured." Others have said, "It's all my fault, I'm to blame for what has happened to me." Some of us have even come to the conclusion that we are being punished for all our past mistakes and we deserve all that has happened to us.

There isn't one among us that is stupid. Nor is there any one of us who is being punished for all we may think we have done in the past. The fact is, one day we were injured and our lives had to change. That's all. Our circumstances are much the same as the rest of us with chronic pain. We are the victims of circumstance and we cannot truly blame ourselves for that. Do I continue to blame myself for my circumstances today?

Higher Power, Please help me learn how to not blame myself for my injury and my circumstances. Help me accept that I am a victim of circumstances and that is all.

Higher Power, please help me cope with my pain today!

If you have not yet met the enemy within, be patient. It is waiting quietly within us for the right time to introduce itself. Our negative self is the enemy. It's the self that tells us things like "You can't do that, you've failed all your life and you are sure to fail this time." It tells us we're worthless and others will never like us because we have chronic pain and we're half the person we used to be. This is the enemy, the one who can direct us to immediate failure and shame.

Today, we have a choice to say "No, no more." I know who and what you are and I will no longer listen to you. You have kept me in your cage for too long. From here on out I will challenge your every word and I will be the one who wins. For you are the enemy. Do I listen to my enemy within?

Higher Power, please help me confront my negative thoughts today.

Higher Power, please help me cope with my pain today!

223

A hug is a wonderful thing. We can give them just about anywhere, at any time, and they are practically free. All that is asked from us, is that we extend our arms and be willing.

For those of us with chronic pain, a hug can do many things. It can cheer us up. It can say, "I love you," or "I'll miss you, come back soon," or "I understand. I understand you have pain and know where you have been. I will be here with you and I will comfort you as best I can." A hug to us can be the beginning of healing our hearts and souls and our pain. Have I given someone or received a hug today?

Higher Power, please help me put down my barriers and give someone a hug today.

Higher Power, please help me cope with my pain today!

224

I know you're in pain and I would do anything to remove it, but I cannot. I feel your hopelessness and powerlessness but I also feel your sense of hope. The hope that someday you will be able to manage your pain and that someday you will feel life is worth living. I pray your past will be overcome by acceptance, not bitterness and blame.

I know you're frightened by the future and terrified of your past. I know that with time you will become excited and look forward to the future with anticipation. I pray your past will become a tool for learning and your fears of financial problems will someday end. I know some people may not understand what you have been through, or what you have done. But I can help them understand.

I know all about you and I know about your pain. I know I care about you and I know all you need to do is ask and I will be here for you. Do I know the friend within myself?

Higher Power, please guide me to my friend within. Please help me understand and accept myself and my pain today.

Higher Power, please help me cope with my pain today!

Learning to cope with and manage our pain has it's own set of rules. Just like any other rules, there are some we will like and some we won't. But for our best chance of success, we must learn to live our lives by these new rules.

Our rules are simple. We can't afford to live in our past, nor can we live in the future. We must come to accept who we are and learn to live our lives according to our limitations. But most importantly, we must strive daily to improve our skills towards managing our pain. By practicing these new rules and others that have proven successful for us, it is sure to bring about change in our lives that may not have seemed possible. Am I willing to accept these new rules or do I want to live by my old ones?

Higher Power, please grant me the courage and faith to move forward and learn how to live by my new set of rules.

Higher Power, please help me cope with my pain today!

Learning to trust ourselves and others will be a major issue for many of us in our recovery. What we had once trusted ourselves to do, we are no longer capable of doing. What was once sound judgement on our behalf, we no longer trusted. Others we had grown to trust, were fading away. We began building walls around ourselves. We had told ourselves we would never trust again.

Trusting ourselves and others again can be a difficult task, but it is possible. In the beginning, we may tend to retreat back to our safe and comfortable ways. This is okay. All we are asked is to be willing to take the risks we are comfortable with each day. Nothing more. Do I trust myself and others today?

Higher Power, please help me learn how to trust myself and others today.

Higher Power, please help me cope with my pain today!

The fog clears when we have come to accept our situations and not before. Some of us get restless and we want to know everything today. We want to know what job we will have, how much money we will make, when our pain will go away, and when we will begin to feel like our old selves again.

We can be as restless as we want to be but we still won't have our answers until the fog clears. For some, this uncertainty will clear faster than it will for others. For those who insist on being impatient, it may seem to take even longer, but the fog will eventually clear. Today, we must be patient, pray, and be prepared for what we may find when the fog does clear. Am I practicing patience while waiting for the fog to clear?

Higher Power, please help me accept that eventually the fog will clear and that I may be pleasantly surprised at what I see.

Higher Power, please help me cope with my pain today!

By now many of us have either been to a support group for people with chronic pain or we are aware of their existence. But just what are these meetings all about? A M.E.E.T.I.N.G. consists of learning ways to manage our pain and sharing our experiences, strengths, and hopes with each other. It is a place to evaluate ourselves, to look within ourselves and to explore the many feelings we may have. A meeting is a place where we learn tolerance for others and patience with ourselves. It is a place to explore new ideas and to find the necessary support we need. It is a place where we can gain knowledge and wisdom from others who have gone before us. Lastly, it is a place of togethernesses. A place where we can come and get the strength we need to continue on in over recovery a day at a time. Do I go to meetings?

Higher Power, please guide me to that special group so I may receive all that is awaiting me today.

Higher Power, please help me cope with my pain today!

AUGUST

If we neglect to manage our pain, chances are it will take us a little at a time. At first, we may begin to lose our physical capabilities. What once seemed effortless, can become an all day affair. Our flare-ups have begun leading us to setbacks rather than as opportunities for growth.

As our physical capabilities decline our emotional health follows. Our attitude and outlook on our recovery begins to fade from one of hope to hopelessness. We become less and less centered on the world around us and more and more consumed with our pain. We have once again become prisoners of our pain.

Our final loss is our spirituality. As in the beginning, we ask our Higher Power, why me? What did I do to deserve this? What we have neglected has begun taking us a little at a time. Do I believe my pain can take me a little at a time?

Higher Power, please give me the strength to work on my recovery a little at a time today. Help me realize that by neglecting my recovery, I can lose it all a little at a time.

Higher Power, please help me cope with my pain today!

In the beginning, it seemed as if we ran out of choices. Our pain consumed and controlled our every thought and action. For many of us, our choices ceased the day we were injured.

As we begin managing our pain, we will discover we have unlimited choices that face us. They may not be the choices we would have picked, but they are choices and that's more than many of us had or ever expected to have. We must remember that we will always have a choice and another path to follow in our recovery. It will be our attitude and outlook towards these choices that will make our difference. Do I see I have unlimited choices today?

Higher Power, please help me become grateful for the choices that you have given me today. Help me accept these choices into my life with a positive attitude.

Higher Power, please help me cope with my pain today!

We live in a society in which we are constantly judged on whether we are successful or whether we fail. Seldom are we judged for the effort we have put forth or given credit for our intentions.

When we begin learning how to manage our pain, most of us will proceed with the purest of intentions. We will constantly be experimenting with new techniques. Some will work for us and others will not. This does not mean that we have failed. If we are to be judged, it is only to be on the merits of whether we have put forth the effort. When it comes to chronic pain, the only way we can fail is not to try. Do I think of myself as a failure today?

Higher Power, help me realize the only way I can fail today is not to try.

Higher Power, please help me cope with my pain today!

Do we know what causes us to have a flare-up? What causes us to slip backwards or what causes us to snap at others without notice? If we don't know we are sure to learn.

As we begin to manage our pain, we will come to know just what our danger points are and how to react to them. This will be a trial and error process. It may be painful at times and humorous the next. We may push ourselves beyond our limits one day and be afraid to try the next. But the more familiar we become with our pain and our bodies, the easier it will be to recognize and respond to our danger points. Have I learned what my danger points are today?

Higher Power, please help me become aware of what my danger points are today.

Higher Power, please help me cope with my pain today!

There is no room for arrogance when dealing with chronic pain. We can't afford to pretend we know or have all the answers. Nor can we afford to become self-centered and think everyone owes us because we were injured. Nor can we allow ourselves to be so consumed by our pride today that we resist help from others.

An attitude of arrogance for those of us with chronic pain is sure to destroy all that we have worked for and possibility our futures. What is my attitude like today?

Higher Power, please help me change my attitude of arrogance to one of willingness and acceptance.

Higher Power, please help me cope with my pain today!

We can't help but to be excited about our new way of life. We have made plans and we're giving it our all. Suddenly we discover our energy has run out. We wonder what has gone wrong. We realize that we have forgotten to pace ourselves. Our once vigorous energy level has not had time to rebuild itself, yet our minds thought otherwise.

Most likely, we can't fix our past or determine our future in one day. We must relax and enjoy our new found way of life and set a pace that is comfortable for us. Everything will get done and unfold in it's time. Tomorrow will arrive when the sun comes up and not before. Am I pacing my program today?

Higher Power, please help me relax and pace my program today. Help me realize all things will get done in their time and not mine.

Higher Power, please help me cope with my pain today!

Many of us enter our recovery with the attitude and belief it will be flawless. We will manage our pain perfectly, we will exercise daily and we will pray at specific times each morning. Our recovery will be perfect. We have forgotten two things. One is we are human and two, chronic pain has it's own way of making perfectionists humble. We will never work a flawless or perfect recovery program. There will always be elements of surprise and situations that will remind us we are far from perfect.

All we are asked to do today is our best. Nothing more nothing less. But most importantly, we will be asked to accept ourselves for what we can do and not for what we think we should be and should do. Do I know there will be flaws in my recovery?

Higher Power, please help me accept my recovery program for what it is today.

Higher Power, please help me cope with my pain today!

In our new life we have many goals and tasks to accomplish. We are excited and filled with hope, but where do we begin? We begin with first things first.

We begin with our physical, emotional, and spiritual health. This is to be our foundation for recovery. Without a clear understanding and working knowledge in these areas, we have very little to work with. The chances of moving ahead and enjoying what recovery has to offer becomes limited. Before all else today, we must begin with first things first. Have I put first things first in my recovery today?

Higher Power, help me realize that I must attend to first things first today if I am to build a firm foundation for my recovery.

Higher Power, please help me cope with my pain today!

In our new life we will be faced with many choices. We will come to realize there are no good or bad choices, just choices. We make a decision based on what we know and then we live with the consequences of our actions.

However, many of us will expect every choice we make to turn out in our favor. We may have forgotten many of the choices we are faced with today are unfamiliar to us. We have chronic pain and with this comes a new life-style with new choices.

We must remember two things today. One is, if we do not take risks and make choices, we are sure to remain silent without signs of growth. Two is, today we have the opportunity to make choices. For many of us there was a time when we had no choice. Have I made any choices today?

Higher Power, help me realize my choices are neither good nor bad, but I must live with the consequences of them.

Higher Power, please help me cope with my pain today!

We must try to stay in today and not reach forward to the future or search desperately for our past.

We must try to manage our pain to the best of our ability and accept any temporary setbacks as inevitable.

We must focus our mind on the positive and not dwell on the negative.

We must try to accept reality for what it is. We must try to change the things we can and accept the things we can't.

For today, we must thank our Higher Power for all we have accomplished and for all that has been given to us. For all we truly have is today. Am I living only for today?

Higher Power, thank you for today.

Higher Power, please help me cope with my pain today!

Denial is not a canal in Egypt. Nor is it a healthy behavior for those of us with chronic pain. When we begin denying how our pain has affected our jobs, our families, our finances and our lives in general, we are headed for danger. We have been walking through our lives blinded from the truth and the reality of our circumstances.

When our denial no longer works for us, we are sure to be faced with all that we have been running from. This will be the time for truth and acceptance. A time to admit all that is taking place in our lives and to begin to accept all for what it is. Today it is our time to seek our truth and stop denying who we are and all that surrounds us. It is time we start looking for our answers rather than running from them. Do I live in denial or am I searching for my answers?

Higher Power, please lead me from the darkness of my denial to the light of your truth.

Higher Power, please help me cope with my pain today!

Somewhere between life's extremes lies a point of balance for each of us. Before we learned to manage our pain and our life's situations, most of us were going from one extreme to the other. We were either feeling as low as we possibly could or we were scraping ourselves off the ceiling.

In our recovery, we must strive each day for our point of balance. We can no longer afford to let ourselves go to the extremes we had in the beginning. Today we have much more to lose and our journey back could be much more difficult than before. When we walk towards our point of balance today, we are coming one step closer to avoiding our return to the extremes we had once lived in. Do I go to the extremes today?

Higher Power, please help me strive for my point of balance today.

Higher Power, please help me cope with my pain today!

Many of us have tried running away from our troubles only to find they were waiting when we had returned. Our pain was no different. We ran as far and as fast as we could hoping it would go away, but it had always returned. Chances are, we will never out run our troubles or our pain. They have become a part of our lives and it is in our best interest to accept them as such.

Today we have a choice. We can continue running or we can begin to seek the positive from our pain and troubles. When we are open-minded and we have the willingness to learn from our pain and troubles, we are sure to find the positive that lies within. Have I turned my pain and troubles into something positive today?

Higher Power, please help me search out the positive that lies within my pain and troubles.

Higher Power, please help me cope with my pain today!

Wishing is our desire or yearning for a specific possession or event to happen. Let's face it, most of us make wishes at one time or another. But how many of these wishes come true? We all wished countless times for our pain to go away, yet it is still with us. We also wished our lives would go back to the way they were, but they didn't. The point is, wishing is a desire and things do not materialize on desire alone. Action on our behalf is needed. When our wish to change something is strong enough action usually follows and change soon occurs. Do I wish for things to happen without taking action?

Higher Power, please help me take action today and not wish my life away.

Higher Power, please help me cope with my pain today!

Yesterday we may have moved mountains but today we may have to settle for moving hills. We are not the same as we were yesterday. Te expect the same results from ourselves is not fair.

As we go through today, we may not accomplish as much as we did yesterday. Nonetheless we still deserve the same credit is if we had.

For the little things we do we can stand tall, be proud, and give ourselves all the credit in the world, for we have put our best foot forward. Some of us will always want to do more because that's our nature. But for today, we can be proud for the little things we do. Have I learned I don't always need to be the best?

Higher Power, please help me be grateful for the little things I do.

Higher Power, please help me cope with my pain today!

There are only 24 hours in a day and so many tasks we can accomplish. Yet many of us push ourselves to the point of exhaustion trying to do it all. The results are usually more anxiety, increased pain or even a re-injury, and less serenity. We must ask ourselves, "Is what we're doing worth these kinds of consequences?"

It is up to us to pace ourselves and take the time we need to rest our mind and bodies. As our recovery progresses, we will come to realize this decision is our responsibility. Others will not ask or push us to take a time out. Rather they will ask that we do more. Do I take the time my mind and body needs to heal today?

Higher Power, please help me realize that I don't need to do it all today. Help me learn to recognize when I need a time out.

Higher Power, please help me cope with my pain today!

Many others like ourselves suffer from chronic pain each day. The degree of despair varies within each of us. Nonetheless, it is despair and nonetheless, others need our prayers as we need theirs.

We're not talking about prayers for a new car or to win the lottery. We're talking about prayers of acceptance of one's condition. Prayers for courage and willingness and prayers for growth. Prayers for giving and receiving support and prayers that no others will every need to endure the pain and despair that we have. Do I pray for others today?

Higher Power, please help me realize we are all one, the ones who have chronic pain, and that I need their prayers as they do mine.

Higher Power, please help me cope with my pain today!

Some of us have yet to totally surrender to our pain. We're clinging to every piece of control that is left. We are consumed with anger and self-pity. We continue to blame ourselves, our Higher Power, and everyone around us for our injury. Acceptance of it all is the furthest thing from our hearts. We're going in circles like a merry-go-round and we feel we can't get off.

Today, we have the power to end our suffering and begin a new life. To get off our merry-go-round and stay off. But first we must surrender to our pain and our condition. Above all, we must grow to accept our situations and to make peace with ourselves. Have I had enough suffering today?

Higher Power, please show me how to end my suffering today. Help me realize there are others who can help me if I ask.

Higher Power, please help me cope with my pain today!

Many of us were severely wounded by our injury and our pain. We began wondering if our lives would ever be returned to normal. We were like a bird with it's wings broken. We hopped around in fear and confusion. We had lost our ability to go at will and ultimately to protect ourselves.

But as our recovery progressed, many of us began to grow a new pair of wings. They were wider and stronger. They were grown from wisdom and experience. They were more than we had hoped to find, but they were just what we needed to begin our new journey. Have I began to grow and develop what I need to begin my new journey?

Higher Power, please grant me what I need to begin my journey today.

Higher Power, please help me cope with my pain today!

To keep the gifts we have been given, we must give them to others in need. We must share our strengths, hopes and personal adventures with others like ourselves. There will be some who refuse any help from us and continue to believe they can do it all themselves. We can't help but feel sad for them and move ahead.

We're not forgetting them, we're practicing patience. They are not yet ready and all our best intentions will not change their attitudes. We will be there for them when they are ready for what we have to give. In the mean time, there are many others who want our help now. We can move ahead to them and help them find what they need and patiently wait for the others. Am I willing to move ahead and help others in need?

Higher Power, please help me learn to move ahead and help others in need. Help me never to forget those who are not yet willing to accept help from others.

Higher Power, please help me cope with my pain today!

The all American cure has been, "take two of these and call me in the morning". Unfortunately, that has also been the case for many of us with chronic pain. There came a point when many health care professionals and alike didn't know what else to do to help relieve our pain, except to give us two of something.

As a result, many of us have become chemically dependent. We became certain we cannot go through one day, let alone the rest of our lives without some type of medication that will attempt to ease our pain. For some this will be their pattern for life. Others will discover they can learn to manage and cope with their pain with little or no medication. Have I chosen two of something to help me ease my pain today or have I chosen to manage my pain without medication?

Higher Power, please help me realize there may be another way to cope with my pain. Grant me the courage and the strength to seek this new way.

Higher Power, please help me cope with my pain today!

Those of us with chronic pain have been uncertain about our futures at one time or another and still may be. We're not sure what our pain will be like from one day to the next or how long we will be able to continue with the work we're doing. Others may be wondering how long they can put forth the effort that is required to manage their pain.

At each turning point along our journey, we may be faced with not knowing what lies ahead. We will be asked to move forward with faith and courage. To work towards answering those uncertain questions we may have, and to come to accept there are some answers we may never come to know. Do I have faith when I am faced with the unknown?

Higher Power, please help me come to accept the unknown. Help me have faith that you will always be there to guide me through the known and the unknown.

Higher Power, please help me cope with my pain today!

Accepting new ideas can be a difficult undertaking. It can be even more difficult when it comes to new ideas about managing our pain. We may have tendencies to reject new ideas and play it safe for fear of increasing our pain or the fear of re-injuring ourselves. When we deny or reject new ideas, we are also denying ourselves the possibility of feeling better physically, emotionally, and spiritually.

We know there are no guarantees when trying new ideas, but if what we are doing isn't working, what do we have to lose? If we are seeking relief from our pain and we have a desire for growth, we must begin putting our fears aside and let acceptance and willingness take it's place. Then and only then, will we be truly ready to accept new ideas. Am I accepting of new ideas today?

Higher Power, please help me clear my mind of the fear that stands in my way of accepting new ideas today.

Higher Power, please help me cope with my pain today!

Many of us had a set routine before we were injured. Suddenly our routine was no longer effective and we panicked. We thought we would be doing the same thing for years to come. However, for most of us, our set routine needed to be changed.

Some will want to go back to their old routine, if possible, and some will explore new ones. Whatever our case may be, we can use these opportunities as a chance to grow and expand our talents and interest. This change may be difficult at first, but as we grow we are sure to find our set routine can return. Have I used this opportunity to change my set routine or am I comfortable with the one I have?

Higher Power, help me use this opportunity as a chance to explore my interest and as a chance to change my set routine.

Higher Power, please help me cope with my pain today!

Many of us with chronic pain have been faced with a new beginning and a new direction. Our injuries have dictated that our lives in some shape or form be altered or changed. Many have shouted out in anger, "I want my old life back". While others have come to realize, this truly could be a new beginning.

This can be a chance to move in directions never dreamed possible. A chance to use the many talents we have been unaware of or to return to school and get that degree we have often thought about. This can be the beginning of a new way of life. One where we can know ourselves and others like never before. This can be the new direction and a new beginning. Have I made my choice for a new beginning today?

Higher Power, please help me realize that the choice to begin a new life today is mine.

Higher Power, please help me cope with my pain today!

There are thousands of people who get up each morning to the call of their pain. They truly believe they are the only ones who feel the way they do. Some go about their days, but remain prisoners in the home depressed and hopeless. Some spend hour upon hour thinking of ways to relieve their pain, while others have tragically taken their lives to end theirs. We ask, "How many more will needlessly suffer today?" Am I one who suffers today or am I reaching out to those who suffer?

Higher Power, please take away the suffering and pain of others today. Help me realize how fortunate I am today.

Higher Power, please help me cope with my pain today!

It is time those of us with chronic pain become selfish. It is time to put our recovery and our health first. Knowing when to say yes and when to say no, knowing when to take personal time and knowing when to go to a meeting must become our priority. For many, our lives depend on it.

This does not give us an excuse to avoid our responsibilities or show a lack of respect for others. Being selfish means making sure we take care of ourselves and that we keep our recovery program a priority. To remain healthy we must learn to be selfish and put our recovery first. Do I have my priorities set according to my recovery today?

Higher Power, help me learn how to be selfish with my recovery and keep my respect for others in the process.

Higher Power, please help me cope with my pain today!

One day my pain appeared and it did not go away. It followed me everywhere I went. I thought it would go away just as it did in the past. But it did not. I realized this was different kind of pain than I had felt before. It has been with me throughout the day and into the night. When the morning arrives I still have my pain. It has become my shadow. It doesn't matter if it's sunny, dark or cloudy, my shadow is always there. How do I feel about my pain today?

Higher Power, please help me accept my pain for what it may be today.

Higher Power, please help me cope with my pain today!

Chronic pain usually has it's own way with our self-esteem and our egos, at least in the beginning. Many of us have been brought to our knees only to be reminded we are no longer able to perform tasks we once were able to. As a result, our egos were bruised and our self-esteem crushed.

Many of us took to what was left of our egos and began replaying who we once were and what we were able to do. We desperately wanted to feel whole and complete as we once did. For many of us, this was the only way we knew that would make us feel alive again.

As our recovery progressed, many of us had found that we no longer had to rely on who we once were and what we were able to do to feel good about ourselves. We had come to accept ourselves for who and what we have become today. We had learned through acceptance to avoid our egos. Am I trying to strengthen my self esteem through my ego?

Higher Power, please help me accept myself for who I am today. Help me avoid using my ego to build my self-esteem.

Higher Power, please help me cope with my pain today!

When our pain takes a turn for the worse and our lives seem unmanageable, many of us use this as an excuse to slip backwards. We tell ourselves, "What's the use it's the same old thing, or I can't do this anymore, it requires more effort than I have".

Whatever excuses we may tell ourselves, all we are doing is setting ourselves up to slip backwards. To slip back to the turmoil we had felt in the beginning. When our pain seems unbearable and our lives seem unmanageable, it is time for us to think of solutions, not excuses. Do I make excuses or do I work towards solutions?

Higher Power, please help me replace my excuses with solutions today.

Higher Power, please help me cope with my pain today!

There are a number of us with chronic pain that are no longer considered spring chickens and sometimes we tend to single ourselves out. We tend to use our age as an excuse to say we are worse off than the others.

To those who feel this way, we would love to give you special attention but we cannot. We are all one, the ones who have chronic pain. If we start saying your pain is worse than ours, we are no longer equal and we no longer need to address our pain in the same manner. We will have detached ourselves from others whose support and friendship we may one day want and need. Do I feel my pain is worse than others?

Higher Power, please help me accept that chronic pain has no boundaries. Help me realize that I don't need to use my pain to be special.

Higher Power, please help me cope with my pain today!

SEPTEMBER

When we're in the depths of our pain and despair, we may have had thoughts of suicide, of running away, or even harming others. Some of us acted on these thoughts and others did not. Some were careful in their deliberation and others acted out of impulse. Some of the consequences to our actions became permanent while others were resolvable.

In our recovery, we are assured of thinking many different things about ourselves and others. Some may be pleasant thoughts and others not so pleasant. But we are assured of one thing. That is, we can take action on our thoughts or they can remain just what they are, thoughts. The choice will be ours. Do I act impulsively on my thoughts today or do I think before taking action?

Higher Power, in the midst of my pain or during a day when everything seems unmanageable, please help me take a moment to think before I act.

Higher Power, please help me cope with my pain today!

267

Are we one-hundred percent honest today? Do we tell others what we really think when they ask? Are we honest with ourselves? Are we honest with our feelings? Are we honest about our shortcomings? Are we honest about our limitations? Have we been honest about the consequences of our injury or about how we may have acted out while in pain?

Chances are we have not been one-hundred percent honest with ourselves and others. But before we decide to place blame or guilt ourselves, we must remember, only our Higher Power achieves one-hundred percent honesty. All we are asked to do is to strive towards being honest. Is my quality of honesty in tune with my Higher Power?

Higher Power, please help me strive each day to improve the quality of my honesty.

Higher Power, please help me cope with my pain today!

We have every reason in the world to feel sorry for ourselves. Most of us have lost our jobs, material possessions and in some cases ourselves, and we're in constant pain. But what good will feeling sorry for ourselves do us? Will it take our pain away or get our job back? NO. Feeling sorry for ourselves will only keep us from moving forward.

We can't afford to feel sorry for ourselves for any length of time. Our new lives are based on gratitude, not self-pity. For us to move forward, take advantage of our new opportunities and manage our pain with any successes, we must rid ourselves of self pity. Am I feeling sorry for myself today?

Higher Power, please replace a feeling of gratitude where I feel self-pity.

Higher Power, please help me cope with my pain today!

When we're feeling depressed and in emotional turmoil or we're having a hard day, it is our responsibility to pick up the phone and ask for support. Waiting for others to call can be an infinite wait in times of need. At times it's easy to look at the phone and think to ourselves, no one cares or they would call. We ask, "Where are they? Don't they know I'm feeling like this?" Chances are they don't and chances are, staring at the phone will not make it ring.

For some of us, the hardest thing to do is ask for help in time of need. We feel they are our troubles and no one else's. Yet we want the phone to ring. We must cast our fears and pride aside, take the first step in receiving support, and pick up the phone or we will continue to wait for others to call. Do I wait for others to call?

Higher Power, please help me cast away my fears and doubts and to call out when I need support instead of waiting for others to call.

Higher Power, please help me cope with my pain today!

When we were injured our lives most likely came to a screeching halt. However, for most of our friends, their lives continued. Some chose to seek understanding with our situations and others were driven away by fear. We must not be too quick to blame others for their actions. But rather seek understanding and acceptance of their position.

In our recovery, there will be opportunities for re-establishing the friendships that may have faded as time passed. It will be our decision and our responsibility to reach out to our friends. Remember, they may remain afraid of our situations and unwilling to reach out to us. If our decision is to pursue these friendships, it is important that we proceed with an open mind and an eye on our expectations. For today, it is time we visit friends. Have I attempted to visit my friends who have faded away with time?

Higher Power, please help me realize the value of friendships today.

Higher Power, please help me cope with my pain today!

I once again wake up to the sound of creaking as I turn my head from side to side. My back slowly straightens out after a few slow stretches. The sharp stabbing pain slowly diminishes. It is replaced by a constant, irritating pain that will become my partner for the day and much of the night. It will challenge my every move and it will consume my every thought. For this day, I will come to know my pain. As I slowly drifted asleep, I recalled what I knew about my pain from today. I fell to my knees and prayed that somehow I would know less about my pain tomorrow. What do I know about my pain today?

Higher Power, please help me come to know and accept my pain today. The more I know and the deeper my acceptance, the greater chance I have of managing it.

Higher Power, please help me cope with my pain today!

Some of us have been called the hopeless ones. The ones who have had too many surgeries. The ones whose symptoms progressed beyond control. The ones whose attitudes and outlook on life have been deemed unchangeable. To some, we truly are the hopeless. The ones who stand little chance at regaining control of our lives. The ones who are certain to remain prisoners of our pain.

If there is a chance for failure there is an equal chance for success. Each and every one of us is granted an opportunity for recovery by our Higher Power. It is what we do with this opportunity that matters. Not what others feel our chances may be or what they think we are capable of. Today, we all have an equal chance. In spite of what others may have said or how I feel, do I believe I have an equal chance of recovery?

Higher Power, I truly believe you love me and you will grant me an equal chance at recovery today. I also know it is up to me to do whatever work you ask of me.

Higher Power, please help me cope with my pain today!

Some of us can return to our previous interests and hobbies, while others are not as fortunate. For the unfortunate ones, they have the right to be angry, and yes, feel sorry for themselves. But only for a short time. Part of our recovery and managing our pain is rejoining life and that's what we intend to do.

Sure, we may have said, "All I know is what I USED to do, nothing else." We hear you and we also hear an excuse not to move on. We realize that developing new interests is a risk and it holds it's own fears. But think of the alternative, which is, to slip into self-pity and once again watch life pass us by. Have I discovered I can develop other interests?

Higher Power, please grant me the strength, the willingness, and the courage to seek out other interests and begin living life rather than watching it pass me by.

Higher Power, please help me cope with my pain today!

Patience is not a popular word among those of us with chronic pain. Many things have either been taken away from us or we have watched them slip through our fingers. Sometimes this happened quickly and other times it was slow and painful. As a result, we became impatient with ourselves and all around us. We wanted to get better yesterday and we wanted back what we had lost the day before that.

Unfortunately, life doesn't work that way. We get what we need when we need it and we get what we want when it is available. All the impatience in the world will not change that. If we are to have patience today, we must begin with prayer and acceptance. This will become our key to our past and a belief for our future. Do I practice patience today?

Higher Power, please help me seek patience today. Help me realize all things can come to those who wait.

Higher Power, please help me cope with my pain today!

In our recovery, we are sure to be faced with many new options and decisions. Some we are sure to grasp hold of and others we are sure to reject without a second thought. Some will think that they have all the answers and others will be filled with fear and won't be willing to look at what lies ahead. Whatever the case, we are not practicing open-mindedness. We must keep in mind that open-mindedness is an adventure with unlimited possibilities. But a closed mind will not allow us to discover what is awaiting us. Am I open-minded or have I closed off all possibilities awaiting me?

Higher Power, please help me learn how to be open-minded today. Help me to see the possibilities that lie ahead.

Higher Power, please help me cope with my pain today!

We are truly privileged people. We are the ones who have chronic pain. We are the exceptions. The ones who have learned to cope with our pain and go on with our lives. We are the ones who have risen from our depths of despair to once again be alive and become a complete person again. We are the ones who have been given a second chance at life. Do I feel I am one of the privileged ones today?

Higher Power, please help me realize that I am truly one of the privileged ones today. For I am alive.

Higher Power, please help me cope with my pain today!

Establishing and maintaining balance may not be an easy task for us in the beginning. There are many issues that have yet to be resolved and many feelings unexplored. As a result, our lives and our emotions are sure to change without warning. We must not panic and above all, we must not give up on ourselves.

With prayer and patience we can establish our own balance. We too can come to know serenity and peace. We can learn to cope with our pain and our emotions. But we must be willing to give this process time. To expect total balance overnight is not fair nor realistic. If we want the gifts that lie ahead, we must be willing to do our part today. Have I reached my point of balance today?

Higher Power, please grant me the courage and patience to walk my journey towards establishing balance.

Higher Power, please help me cope with my pain today!

My life now has a different direction. My injury was it's cause. In the beginning it was confusing and extremely painful. I had little hope and no cause to go on living. My pain was unbearable and my depression even worse. I had become a prisoner. I became consumed with self-pity for what I was no longer capable of doing. My friends had moved on and I was alone with my pain. I had tried taking my life, but failed.

Today I have a different direction. It is filled with hope and one of purpose. I no longer have to be alone and consumed by self-pity. It is a direction I could have never imagined I would be taking. But today it has become my direction. Am I willing to explore different directions today?

Higher Power, please guide me in your direction today.

Higher Power, please help me cope with my pain today!

Communicating and expressing ourselves while in pain is not an easy task to accomplish. However, it is an essential one. When we're in pain it's easy to become short with ourselves and others. Ultimately we end up saying things we don't mean and can't take back. Before we condemn ourselves to a life of guilt, we must remember that our thoughts and actions while in pain can be confusing, leaving communication difficult at best.

For us to communicate effectively while in pain, we must learn to step back, gather our thoughts, and then speak. If at first we are not successful, be patient. With practice we can learn to communicate effectively with ourselves and those around us. Do I communicate effectively today?

Higher Power, please teach me how to communicate with myself and others. Help me learn how to ask for what it is I need today.

Higher Power, please help me cope with my pain today!

Most of the time we really don't know just what lies ahead for us. What we do know is that our Higher Power has set a path for each and every one of us to travel. What lies ahead for us, only our Higher Power knows. Our Higher Power has watched over us, loved and cared for us, and has carefully designed our journey to meet our needs and our wants. If we are to truly experience what lies ahead, we must continue to follow the path our Higher Power has set for us. For what lies ahead only our Higher Power knows. Do I put trust and faith in my Higher Power for what lies ahead?

Higher Power, please help me have faith that your path will reveal what lies ahead.

Higher Power, please help me cope with my pain today!

When we have a flare-up or a setback we must admit it to ourselves and when necessary to others. For some of us, our temptation is to tell others we are doing okay for fear of them knowing we have had a slip or taken a step backwards. This can be dangerous behavior. We are allowing our pride and egos to emerge. As a result, we put our physical, emotional and spiritual lives in danger.

We must remember that flare-ups, slips and setbacks are all symptoms of having chronic pain. We are not any less of a person or weak for admitting to our situation. When we have the temptation to hide our condition today, we must ask ourselves if it is our pride or our ego that has flared-up. Do I admit to myself and others when I have had a flare-up or setback?

Higher Power, please help me learn to admit to myself and others when I am not doing so well.

Higher Power, please help me cope with my pain today!

If we are to learn how to manage our pain and continue to grow in our recovery, we must begin focusing on our solutions rather than living in our problems. In order to do this a complete change in attitude is needed. There will be no room for self-pity or the attitude that we are victims and our lives can never change. Solutions demand change and that is what we must do if we are to avoid living in our problems.

Today is time for change. It is time we begin living the solution rather than the problem. Our first step is to recognize our problems. The second step is to make a list of possible solutions to each problem. The third step is we must put these solutions into action. Do I focus on solutions today or my problems?

Higher Power, please grant me the wisdom to see the solutions to my problems today and grant me the courage to take whatever action is needed.

Higher Power, please help me cope with my pain today!

Some of us believe that being assertive is the same as being aggressive. It's not. Being aggressive is being demanding and forceful. This rarely gets our needs or wants met. On the other hand, being assertive is asking for what we want and what we need and it's carried out in a caring and respectful manner.

Our tendency, when in pain, is to be aggressive, demanding and forceful. This accomplishes very little. We stand a far better chance of having our needs met when we're acting in a calm and assertive manner and others will be far more receptive to us. While practicing assertiveness takes patience and an open mind, the results will be well worth the time and effort. Will I practice aggressiveness or assertiveness today?

Higher Power, please help me become less aggressive and more assertive so I may have my needs met today.

Higher Power, please help me cope with my pain today!

When we are experiencing growth we are changing within, and this can be a wonderful thing. However, this process can leave us sitting somewhere in the middle and confused. We know we are not the people we used to be and we're not sure who we will become. But one thing we are certain of and that is our fear. If not overcome, we are sure to gain little growth.

To grow and have change occur in our lives, requires faith and taking a stand on our behalf. A stand that we will not retreat into our old selves in times of hardship. A stand that we will move forward with faith and courage, regardless of fear and uncertainty. To grow and change today, we must first believe our Higher Power will guide us on our journey. Secondly, we must have the willingness to want this change. Am I willing to grow and change today?

Higher Power, please be by my side as I start my journey towards growth and change.

Higher Power, please help me cope with my pain today!

My pain has become my best friend and my worst enemy. It has treated me with gentleness and it has cast pain on me beyond belief. My pain has been predictable and unpredictable. It has had me in tears and it has made me laugh. It has offered hope and it has brought hopelessness. It has been manageable and at times unmanageable. It has aided in addiction and it has brought recovery. It has caused bitterness and blame only to force acceptance and responsibility. My pain has taken away old direction and presented me with new direction. For today, this is some of what I know about my pain. What do I know about my pain today?

Higher Power, please help me learn about my pain today. Help me accept it's gentleness as well as it's unpredictability.

Higher Power, please help me cope with my pain today!

We can all take a moment to congratulate ourselves. We have graduated from the school of hard knocks. We have paid the highest rate of tuition ever. Our pain. The lessons we have learned will not be forgotten. We have spent many hours in pain. We've studied it, asked questions about it, passed and failed it's tests, and at times we've wanted to withdraw from it. But we haven't. We have not given up. For that we can be proud. But there is more learning that lies ahead and more we must share with others, for they need our knowledge and wisdom. Have I learned all about my pain or do I have room for growth?

Higher Power, please help me realize I have more to learn about managing my pain. Help me not to become complacent and pass on my knowledge to others.

Higher Power, please help me cope with my pain today!

We had met with little or no warning. It was instant attraction. Our courtship had lasted seconds. We were to be married without any possibility of divorce. My pain and I had become one. We would eat together, sleep together, work together and vacation together. We would learn to hate one another and learn to make amends. We would try to run from one another only to be reunited. We would talk for hours on end but never come to any conclusions. But mostly, we would wonder what we would do with each other for the rest of our days to come. What is my relationship with my pain today?

Higher Power, please help me grow to understand and accept my pain.

Higher Power, please help me cope with my pain today!

There are times when we need to stay home and rest. To give ourselves a break. But there are also times when we don't make the choice to stay home. Our bodies make that choice for us. On these days we have the choice to make the best of the situation or we can sit at home, focus on our pain, and feel sorry for ourselves. Our bodies may not work the way we would like them to, but we can control our attitude.

During these days we can catch up on some reading, write those letters we've been meaning to write, call another person we know with chronic pain or just relax to some music. Whatever we do, our objective is to accept that physically we may not be able to totally control what is happening, but mentally we can choose to make the best of our stay at home. What do I do when I stay at home?

Higher Power, please help me make wise use of my time when my day comes to stay home.

Higher Power, please help me cope with my pain today!

We had come together with the expectation of leaving one another. Little did we know, our first embrace would last an eternity. We had become partners with our pain. If we had known in advance who and what our partner was and it's capabilities, chances are we would have requested another. But for today, our partner is our pain. We will come to know it as no other partner before. We will come to learn it's many moves and it's requests for silence. We will learn our pain can be smooth and gentle. But at times it will lead us with vengeance. We will come to know, for today our pain is our partner. Have I accepted my pain today?

Higher Power, please help me accept my pain as my partner today.

Higher Power, please help me cope with my pain today!

The end of a journey is near. I have learned many lessons that were unexpected, and priceless. I have come to know myself and my pain as never before. I have cried and I have laughed. I have wanted to give up and I have been overcome with hope. I have faced fear and I have come to know faith. I have learned about others and I have come to know compassion. But above all, I have learned "the end" is not always the end. It is a completion of one part of life. There are many journeys that lie ahead. The only question that remains is, "Am I willing to take another?" Am I willing to begin another journey today?

Higher Power, from the bottom of my heart and soul, I thank you for walking me through this journey. Please grant me the courage to begin another.

Higher Power, please help me cope with my pain today!

Chronic pain has been known to be the cause of unfulfilled promises. It has taken away the promising careers of many. It has taken away the promises of a new family for some and it has destroyed existing families for others. But it's most unfulfilled promise, is that it has taken the lives of many who had promising lives ahead of them. But with it's unfulfilled promises emerged promise and hope for many others. In some direct or indirect way, many of us have come to understand our own pain and our capabilities. For what was once unfulfilled promises has turned into new direction and hope for many. Have I looked for the positives in my unfulfilled promises?

Higher Power, please grant me the wisdom to seek out the positive lessons with my pain today.

Higher Power, please help me cope with my pain today!

In the beginning, I had tried everything I could to escape the pain and turmoil I was in. I wanted relief. I was sure that I wasn't capable of handling my pain for one more minute, let alone for the rest of my life. I had discovered that when I escaped reality my pain seemed to lessen. But as time passed, I began noticing my pain was following me. No matter where my mind had wandered, my pain soon followed. I had come to realize there was no sense trying to out run my pain. But what else am I to do? Do I try escaping my pain today or am I taking the steps necessary to manage it?

Higher Power, please grant me the courage to begin facing and managing my pain today.

Higher Power, please help me cope with my pain today!

Many of us have thought that our lives were over and that our pain was to keep us prisoners for life. We would surface once or twice a day only to see our world passing us by. As time passed, our awareness and desire for life grew. We realized that there was a whole lot of life for us to live. Our decision was made. We were no longer willing to watch our lives pass by.

Our pain no longer has to be our enemy or hold us prisoners. Rather, we could use our pain to guide us and take advantage of the many directions it has to offer. Do I believe there's a whole lot of life left for me?

Higher Power, please show me there is a whole lot of life left for me to live. Show me how my pain can be my guide rather than my enemy.

Higher Power, please help me cope with my pain today!

Once again I awoke in pain. I have a full day ahead, yet I have no energy, no ambition, and no hope. I ask myself, "Why me? What did I do to deserve this? Why hasn't my life gotten any better?" I'm fed-up. I've had enough. You can have this life. I want my old one back. Can I have it back? I don't think I can. I think I'm stuck with who I am. No, it can't be. What will I do? Where will I go? What will become of me? This can't be happening. I think it is and I think I'm fed-up with it. Am I fed-up with my life today?

Higher Power, please help me find the hope that lies within me.

Higher Power, please help me cope with my pain today!

Some of us can't imagine that we can have any kind of a life with chronic pain. We find it hard to believe that someone with the kind of pain we have can actually be happy, productive, and even content. We have heard of others talk about living this sort of life, but many of us have never seen it for ourselves. If we don't believe this is true, we must look for ourselves.

There are many of us with chronic pain who have succeeded. They have learned to manage their pain, they are reasonably content, and they have come to accept themselves as they are. If we are having troubles believing today, it just may be we need to see for ourselves. Do I believe I can succeed as others with chronic pain have?

Higher Power, please help me believe in the successes of others and to believe that I, too, can succeed just as they have.

Higher Power, please help me cope with my pain today!

OCTOBER

Heat, ice and the rest are considered to be tools of those with chronic pain can turn to in times of flare-ups. Some of us prefer heat, some ice and some the rest.

Whatever our choice, we must keep in mind that every tool we use will not have the same results. However, it is in our best interest to keep an open mind. What we used today may not work tomorrow, but it may be just what we need down the road.

We're not after the quantity of tools in times of flare-ups, rather we're after the quality of their relief. We must not try and impress others with all we know, but rather impress ourselves with what we know works for us. Do I know what works for me?

Higher Power, please help me realize that flare-ups are part of my pain. Help me keep an open mind and become willing to explore all options of managing my pain today.

Higher Power, please help me cope with my pain today!

We all have shortcomings. No one among us is perfect. Yet many of us strive each day to achieve perfection. For others, this may be okay. But for those of us with chronic pain, we cannot afford to hold on to this attitude. Sure, we can strive to do our best, but not for perfection.

For our best chances of success, we must learn to accept and recognize our day to day progress and our imperfections. We may at times want to continue to search out those perfect solutions to our problems, but we must keep in mind there is only one perfect solution to any problem, but there are many excellent solutions to all our problems. Do I strive for progress or perfection today?

Higher Power, please help me work towards progress today and not perfection.

Higher Power, please help me cope with my pain today!

If we have looked out the window lately, we will have seen that life for many others is still going around in spite of us having pain. Many of us had thought a time or two that the world should stop it's existence until we were back to our old selves. But it did not. Most of our family and friends had carried on with their lives as well, but we had remained prisoners of our pain. Is my life continuing to go around or do I remain a prisoner of my pain?

Higher Power, please give me the strength and courage to break free from being a prisoner of my pain. Please show me the way to a new life today.

Higher Power, please help me cope with my pain today!

When we feel desperate we are far from being in control of ourselves emotionally or physically. Our sense of right and wrong is diminished and our behavior becomes reckless. Because of our desperation, we might take risks that will put our physical and emotional selves in great danger. We might be offered a job that we know requires too much lifting, but we are desperate for the money so we take it. Or we may find ourselves in an unhealthy relationship, driven by a desperate need for companionship, and we suffer emotionally and spiritually because of it.

When we find ourselves feeling desperate, we have a choice to react to it or to step back and ask ourselves why we are feeling desperate. Today can be our day to shift from a feeling of desperation to one of hope. Do I feel desperate today?

Higher Power, please help me confront my feelings of desperation today.

Higher Power, please help me cope with my pain today!

If you have chronic pain you have certainly felt frustration at one time or another and we are certain to experience more as our recovery progresses.

At times, managing our pain can seem like threading a needle. The first few misses are expected, but soon after we become more and more frustrated and we give up. We cannot afford to take this attitude toward managing our pain and our recovery. We cannot afford to give up all we have worked for because of a few near misses. Nor can we afford to let our frustration dictate the course and intensity of our pain. We are in control of managing our own recovery and the levels of our frustration today. Do I let my frustration block my progress in recovery?

Higher Power, please help me learn how to cope with my frustration today. Help me realize that I have a choice on how I react to those near misses in my life.

Higher Power, please help me cope with my pain today!

Learning to manage our pain will most likely be a life long process. We will be constantly experimenting. Trying this and trying that, while putting together different combinations to see what's effective and what's not. This is sure to require courage, willingness, and patience. Most of the time our answers will not be found on the first try but eventually we are sure to find what we are looking for.

As time passes, we must realize that what has been so effective for us, may fade away and no longer work. Our bodies are constantly changing and they may require us to change our methods as well. When we're willing to change and grow with our bodies, chances are we will be pleasantly surprised by the results. Do I experiment when managing my pain or do I think the same comfortable methods will always work?

Higher Power, please grant me the courage and willingness to explore other options of managing my pain today.

Higher Power, please help me cope with my pain today!

Sleep? What is that we ask. Many of us have not seen a full night's sleep in weeks, months, and even years. Our pain has become our night's companion, our inner alarm clock. When the sun rises, we're immediately reminded we had no sleep and no rest. Our bodies are tired yet we have a full day ahead.

We realize we have begun deteriorating physically, mentally and spiritually. Our attitude and outlook on life slowly worsens. We are fading into the night as the days hold less and less meaning. We have had no sleep and no rest. Do I get enough sleep to face the next day?

Higher Power, please help me seek out new ways to rest my mind and body.

Higher Power, please help me cope with my pain today!

The blackness of night can be the most difficult time for those of us with chronic pain. While the day has taken it's toll, the darkness brings loneliness, fear and the pain that always follows the day's events. We wonder if anybody is out there, if anybody cares. We say to ourselves, "I need somebody tonight, someone who will hold me and tell me it will be okay. Someone to take away the loneliness and fear, and someone to ease my pain."

We take to the phone. There is no answer. There is no one there for us. We fall to our knees and say, "I need somebody tonight." The phone rings and while on our knees we say, " Thanks God for being that somebody tonight."

Do I need somebody tonight and if so, do I know who that somebody is for me?

Higher Power, today I know and trust that when I need somebody you will always be there.

Higher Power, please help me cope with my pain today!

306

When we decide we no longer want to be prisoners of our pain and we are willing to go to any lengths for the help we need, we are ready to come out of the dark. Ready to leave that place that has held our lives and dreams captive. That place that has stolen relationships from us and has slowly taken our dignity away.

Coming out of the dark and taking back our lives is no small task. It will require courage and the best of our efforts each day. We are sure to be faced with new challenges and asked to take risks we may be afraid to take. But by being willing to go to any lengths we are protecting ourselves from returning to our once unforgiving darkness and granted the opportunity for growth. Have I made a decision to break out of my darkness?

Higher Power, please give me the courage to break out of my darkness and despair. Help me face whatever challenges that I may face today.

Higher Power, please help me cope with my pain today!

Many of us have slipped backwards several times and we were able to return successfully with little harm. Yet others were not fortunate enough to return as easily, if at all. When it comes to slipping, we can't afford to take chances. Just because others have taken several steps backwards and returned doesn't mean we will be as fortunate.

For some of us, slipping can take us right back to the depression and despair we had known in the beginning leaving us feeling hopeless once again. To avoid slipping back to our despair, we must constantly be aware of our emotional, physical, and spiritual conditions. When we neglect these areas for any length of time, we are in danger of slipping so far back that we become one of the less fortunates. Do I avoid slips today?

Higher Power, please help me prepare myself so I am not the next one to slip. Grant me the courage to reach out and help those around me who are less fortunate and do slip.

Higher Power, please help me cope with my pain today!

Those of us with chronic pain have at one time or another thought of ourselves as victims. That's okay, we are. We are victims of circumstance. But when we're consumed with the notion we are always going to be victims, we have crossed the line into genuine self-pity.

As we continue to project our self-pity outward, others are sure to feel sorry for us as well. We will have become the pitiful victims of our circumstances. We will have knowingly or unknowingly created a world of self-pity through our pain and those around us. We then truly have become victims of our own self-pity. Am I consumed with self-pity today?

Higher Power, please take away my self-pity today. Help me realize that I am a victim of circumstance and not a victim of my own self-pity.

Higher Power, please help me cope with my pain today!

309

Today we may be undecided or even confused when it comes to managing our pain. Some want to know if it works and others want to know how much effort it will take. Some want to know if they can have their old life back and others want to know where they might go. Some want to know what will be asked of them and others are too frightened to know.

For some, their decision was made for them. They would learn or they would die. For others, this has become our moment of decision. Have I made my decision?

Higher Power, please give me the courage to make my decision today.

Higher Power, please help me cope with my pain today!

By now most of us have discovered that we do not have to go through recovery and try to manage our pain alone. We know there are many others just like us who need us as much as we need them. Our greatest and most dominant link is that we have chronic pain and that we are willing to go to any lengths to cope with it.

Finding fellowship with others who have chronic pain is only a phone call away. But this may as well be a thousand mile journey by foot if we are afraid and unwilling to reach out to others. In many cases, it will be up to us to search out this fellowship we want and in most cases, need. Have I found fellowship with others who have chronic pain?

Higher Power, please direct me towards finding fellowship with others who have chronic pain. Help me be the one to take the first step today.

Higher Power, please help me cope with my pain today!

Managing our pain is one aspect of our recovery, but it is hardly enough. We must strive to improve our emotional and spiritual lives as well. Most of us have been taken so far down emotionally that all we have come to know is fear and anger. Somewhere along the way we had lost our ability to care about ourselves and our futures. Our emotions had slowly slipped away from us.

Our spiritual lives were no different. We wondered why our Higher Power could have let this happen to us. We wondered what we could have done to deserve this kind of pain. Over time nothing had changed with our situation, so we abandoned our spirituality for anger and resentment.

Without our emotional and spiritual lives in order, we have little chance of being successful at managing our pain and experiencing growth. Today, managing our pain is hardly enough. Have I begun putting my emotional and spiritual life in order?

Higher Power, please help me realize that managing my emotional and spiritual life is just as important as managing my pain.

Higher Power, please help me cope with my pain today!

No matter how much we try to be or want to be alone with our pain, we must deny ourselves of doing so. Our pain and troubles are too great to bear alone. Many of us have tried living alone with our pain at one time or another and we have found ourselves frightened and discouraged. We had made little progress in coping with our pain and were becoming more depressed. We were living alone.

If we have not done so, we are faced with one of our most crucial decisions thus far. Do we retreat and live alone with our pain, or do we pray for the courage and guidance to seek out support from others? Today the decision is ours. Do I live alone with my pain?

Higher Power, please guide me to that place where others can give me support and help me cope with my pain.

Higher Power, please help me cope with my pain today!

We're all traveling down the same path. The path of recovery. We're searching for a common goal; learning to cope with our pain one day at a time.

For this to materialize, we must keep this goal a priority. We must always remember that we are not alone. There are many others who are willing to help. All we need to do is ask.

When we lose our willingness to keep our recovery a first priority and to reach out and ask for help, we have strayed off our path and begun a different journey. One that may bring us more pain and loneliness than we had known before.

If we find ourselves trying to take a short cut or straying off our path, it is time to ask ourselves what our goals and priorities are for today. Have I made my recovery a priority today?

Higher Power, please help me keep my recovery a priority today. Help me reach out to others when I need help.

Higher Power, please help me cope with my pain today!

Taking an immediate inventory in the midst of a crisis can be a great benefit to those of us with chronic pain. By stepping back and assessing our situation, we can reduce our chances of physically harming ourselves or carelessly making a decision that is not in our best interest. We may also find that by stepping back, we may better evaluate our situation and our alternatives.

Learning to take immediate inventories will require patience and the willingness to continue to practice until it has become second nature to us. Do I take immediate inventories today or do I make decisions without assessing my situation?

Higher Power, please show me now to relax and step back and take an immediate inventory today.

Higher Power, please help me cope with my pain today!

315

Many of us have thought that the way we are today is the way we will always be. Some have thought they would remain depressed and their pain would control their lives until their last breath. Change for many of us was beyond comprehension.

As our minds begin to clear and we begin to manage our pain, we will come to realize that change is not only possible, it is inevitable. By giving our best effort each day and believing that change can occur in our lives, we are sure to move forward and experience change. Do I believe that change can occur in my life?

Higher Power, please help me believe that change can occur in my life and I no longer need to live in fear.

Higher Power, please help me cope with my pain today!

With little or no warning our back slips out and our leg gives way. Just as we were going to go out for the evening, we are greeted by a surprise attack of pain. We wonder what's next. How many times is this going to happen? Our attitude starts to fade but we recover quickly. We remember hearing that this too shall pass. Chances are this is a temporary flare-up. If we hold steady and practice what we have learned, we are sure to make it through this.

There is no guarantee or freedom from surprise attacks. They may come and go at any time. But there is a guarantee that by putting what we have learned into practice, we can work our way through these surprise attacks and go on with our lives. Am I prepared to cope with my surprise attacks?

Higher Power, help me realize these surprise attacks are temporary flare-ups. Help me realize I have the ability to work through them.

Higher Power, please help me cope with my pain today!

Learning how to manage our pain will not be enough for most. We may need to educate ourselves as well. Seeking education about our specific condition or how to properly exercise or how chronic pain can effect us emotionally, can influence and support our efforts in recovery.

By educating ourselves, we are sure to gain confidence and be better prepared to make the many decisions that lie ahead. With most things, the less we know about them the more fearful we are. Chronic pain is no different.

Today we must become students of chronic pain. We must keep up on the latest treatments for managing our pain and take an active role in our recovery. Our active role is sure to equal a productive outcome. Do I continue to educate myself about chronic pain or do I feel I know it all?

Higher Power, please help me take an active role in my recovery today.

Higher Power, please help me cope with my pain today!

318

We all make up excuses here and there when we want to avoid doing something. That's normal. But when our excuses start multiplying and we begin believing them, our lives are clearly in danger.

Our excuses, whether based from our fear, our pain or our unwillingness, will eventually take control of our lives and become our dictator. They will deny us all opportunities for fulfilling our wants, our needs and our dreams. Our excuses will have become an inner conscious that will haunt us until we have found another way of coping with our lives. Do I use excuses to avoid making decisions today?

Higher Power, please help me face my fears, my pain, and my unwillingness so I no longer can use them as excuses.

Higher Power, please help me cope with my pain today!

For many of us with chronic pain, finding happiness in today seems effortless. We have come to feel grateful just to be alive. We have not forgotten what our lives were like before we began managing our pain and we certainly know how our lives have changed since then.

But there are others who have yet to find a trace of happiness. Each day is a continuous struggle to rise to their feet and begin their day. They have yet to feel gratitude and they are living in a time where happiness seems to be and endless possibility. Am I finding happiness in today?

Higher Power, please help me find a trace of happiness today.

Higher Power, please help me cope with my pain today!

Those of us with chronic pain certainly have every right to be angry. But we don't have the right to take our anger and frustration out on everyone who crosses our path. Some have come to the conclusion that because we are in pain and our lives have been altered without our permission, it is okay to take our feelings out on others. This is not so.

We have the right, and obligation, to step aside and determine why we are angry and at whom we are angry. We have the right to express our anger, but in an appropriate manner. We have the right and obligation to treat others the way we want to be treated. For today, we have the right. Do I use the rights I have to express my anger today?

Higher Power, please help me cope with whatever unresolved anger I may have today in an appropriate manner.

Higher Power, please help me cope with my pain today!

In the beginning, many of us tended to live in the past. We continually relived those memories of what we once were able to do. We relied on these memories to help us feel better about ourselves and to avoid the present. For many of us, our lives had become a continual tape of memories.

We somehow had crossed that line where memories had been recalled for pleasure not survival. Many of us began believing that we could not exist without recalling what we used to be like and what we had once accomplished. Without those memories, we had felt empty and as if our life had no value. How do I use my memories today?

Higher Power, when I look back on my life, please help me keep those thoughts as memories and not as a means of survival. Please help me accept that I am valued and that I am a worthwhile person just as I am today.

Higher Power, please help me cope with my pain today!

We have logged many miles on our new journey. We have traveled many roads that were unfamiliar to us, yet we haven't gotten lost. We may have been side-tracked, or delayed from time to time, but not lost. For that we can be proud and grateful. However, we have miles to go as our new lives have just begun. The road of hopes, dreams, happiness and serenity have yet to be taken. We still have many miles to go.

Today we have the choice to stop with what miles we have logged, or to continue down unexplored roads. Am I content with my miles logged or do I want to explore my untraveled roads?

Higher Power, I thank you for the miles we have logged together and I ask that you be with me, for I have many more miles to go on my new journey.

Higher Power, please help me cope with my pain today!

Many with chronic pain have come and gone. Some have taken their own lives and others have passed on naturally. Regardless, they are not to be forgotten. In their own way they have shown others what to do and what not to do, how to live and how not to live.

When we work with others who have chronic pain, we can respectfully use those who are gone as examples. Not by showing how they were right or wrong in their life's doings, but rather what they have done for us and shown us. These are the ones who are gone, but not forgotten. Do I respect and remember those who went before me?

Higher Power, please help me learn from those who have gone before me. Please help me have respect for them and never forget them.

Higher Power, please help me cope with my pain today!

Our responsibility for helping others who have chronic pain is, when anyone, anywhere, reaches out their hand for help, we are to be there. Some may be thinking, you've got to be kidding. We're not. When we were in our depths of despair, we desperately wanted someone who cared, but most importantly, we wanted someone who understood what we were going through. For most of us there was no one. We were alone until we found others who were like us.

For those who are alone and are reaching out for help, it is up to us to extend our hand and help. We must give of ourselves to keep what has been given so freely to us. Do I give of myself to those who need my help?

Higher Power, please help me give freely of myself to those who are suffering from their pain. Help me realize we are all one, the ones who have chronic pain.

Higher Power, please help me cope with my pain today!

Many of us arrived at the point where our pain totally consumed us. It wasn't that we wanted it that way, but because we knew no other way. Our pain directed our every action. In the process, we hurt ourselves and we hurt others. As time passed, we had been overcome by guilt. We felt guilty for our behavior towards others and for what we were no longer able to do. We felt we were no longer the husband or wife or partner we thought we should be. Some of us have even felt responsible for our injury.

Whatever our case, it is time to let go of our guilt. By taking responsibility for our past actions and confronting our feelings of guilt, we will come to realize a new freedom and a new happiness without guilt. Do I feel guilty about my past actions?

Higher Power, please help take away the guilt that is within me. Show me what I need to do today to become at peace with myself and others.

Higher Power, please help me cope with my pain today!

As we begin our recovery we must also begin setting new boundaries. We will be starting a new life with new limitations and new priorities. Setting our boundaries accordingly will be a must. We cannot afford to be ambivalent about where we stand or about what we allow and don't allow others to do to us or for us. Today, we must set our boundaries with clarity. For they will become our new guide and our new rules for living. Have I begun setting my new boundaries today?

Higher Power, please help me establish my new boundaries and grant me the strength and the willingness to abide by them.

Higher Power, please help me cope with my pain today!

If we had a dollar for everytime we have asked, "Why me? Why do I have to have pain? Why can't I have my old life back?" we would be close to being millionaires. Unfortunately there are no easy answers for these and the many other questions we may have. For some of us this will not suffice. We will search the world over and over trying to have our questions answered. Others will seek out their Higher Power, not so much for answers, but for acceptance. It is through this acceptance that many of us may come to find our answers. But if not, we are sure to find a peace of mind and calmness like never before. Do I know there are no easy answers when it comes to my pain?

Higher Power, please help me learn to accept the known and the unknown today.

Higher Power, please help me cope with my pain today!

Some of us have a harder time than others managing our pain during the winter months. It seems the cold comes howling through our bodies leaving behind an echoing pain that can last for months. We may feel as if the progress we have made has failed us once again and that we are slowly slipping backwards. Don't panic. You have hit the ice age.

For those whose pain rises during the winter months, it is time we change our routines. It is time we prepare ourselves for the winter ahead. We may consider taking in extra support meetings, moving more of our activities indoors, and yes, even exercising more than we normally do. By preparing ourselves and experimenting with different techniques, we will be one step ahead of the ice age. Am I prepared for the winter ahead?

Higher Power, please help me be willing to change my routine for the winter ahead. Grant me the strength to do whatever it takes to make the winter ahead manageable.

Higher Power, please help me cope with my pain today!

NOVEMBER

Sometimes we can fall into a pattern of over-protecting ourselves from reinjury and we forget to live life. Unfortunately there is only so much protecting we can do. After that, there is really nothing we can do or nothing we have control over. If for some reason we re-injure ourselves, or we have a flare-up, it is up to us to decide if and when we will move forward.

Our other option is to fade into our past and let life pass us by. Remember, by over-protecting ourselves, we can go further back. Possibly ending up in our old despair and depression. The next thing we know is we have rebuilt our wall so high that no one can approach us. Do I protect myself to the point that I forget to live my life?

Higher Power, please help me not to protect myself to the point where I forget to live my life.

Higher Power, please help me cope with my pain today!

The world is larger than most of us will ever know, but our corner of the world seems to be just the right size. We have all been given special gifts by our Higher Power and they are to be used to help those around us.

Our personal power is our experience, strength and hope. It is our attitude that we project on others. It is our willingness to reach out to others. It is our ability to recognize that we are not gods. We are those who want to make a difference by using our personal powers. Do I use the gifts my Higher Power has given me to help others?

Higher Power, please help me not to play God today. Help me realize that you have given me the power to make a difference in my corner of the world.

Higher Power, please help me cope with my pain today!

If managing our pain is our goal, then we must start today. Wishing the past never happened or that someone will take our pain away, will get us nowhere. When we keep one foot in yesterday and one in tomorrow, we will never own today. Our experiences will be from yesterday and our pain borrowed from the future. Today will have come and gone without a trace. All that we will have owned is our pain. Do I manage my pain one day at a time?

Higher Power, help me realize that managing my pain requires me to stay in the here and now. By owning today, I am building for a better tomorrow.

Higher Power, please help me cope with my pain today!

Our new life with chronic pain will be filled with chances for us to take. We may fall many times, only to be presented with a chance to rise to our feet and try again. We will have the chance to grow physically, emotionally, and spiritually. We will have the chance to share with others who have chronic pain and meet new friends. We will have more chances and opportunities in our new life that at times may seem overwhelming to us. But we don't need to take every chance or opportunity that is put in our path, nor do we have to take all our chances in one day. Just one chance at a time. Do I take chances in my life today?

Higher Power, please grant me the opportunities and chances you feel I need to take today.

Higher Power, please help me cope with my pain today!

How many times have we said, "I can't do that anymore?" For some things this may be true, for others we don't know unless we try. In our early stages of learning to manage our pain, we remembered every ache and flare-up. We were consumed by fear. When we tried to do something, the result was "I can't." We had found our safety net, a way of protecting ourselves. As we learn to manage our pain, we will better understand our limitations. Our attitude will shift from one of fear to one of, "I might not be able to do that, but I'll try another way." With this change of attitude comes a change in options. Do I say "I can't" to protect myself today?

Higher Power, please help me realize that when I say "I can't" it's for protection and not said out of fear.

Higher Power, please help me cope with my pain today!

What value do I place on my life? Do I feel my life
is worth living? Do I feel I have something to offer
others? Do I feel a purpose in life or do I feel my life is
filled with so much pain, it will never amount to
anything?

Our lives hold whatever value we put on them.
They can be worth as much or as little as we want
them to be. It is our choice. What value does my life
hold today?

Higher Power, please help me realize that the value of
my life is worth everything today.

Higher Power, please help me cope with my pain today!

When we become complacent and forget to work at our recovery, we usually have a pile-up followed by a blow-out. By ignoring our physical, emotional and spiritual condition we are sure to regress to our old ways. This is the beginning of our pile-up.

Our blow-out is the consequences of our actions. Our emotional condition fades. We become irritable and think we can handle everything by ourselves. We refuse to exercise and our pain worsens. The final blow-out comes when we lose contact with our Higher Power. Our serenity and peace of mind fade quickly and we once again feel afraid and alone. Have I become complacent in my recovery?

Higher Power, please help me not to be complacent with my recovery today. Help me realize what consequences lie ahead if I do so.

Higher Power, please help me cope with my pain today!

Perhaps we have gotten ourselves into a mess financially, our creditors are upset and they call more often than we would like. For many of us our first thought is to run or somehow escape. Our second thought may be to stay and face the music, to take responsibility for ourselves. For many, this is a dilemma.

We have found that creditors can be human and somewhat understanding when we come clean and keep in contact with them. But if we run and then come back, we usually have more of a mess than when we left. Many of us may not like taking responsibility for ourselves and we may find it uncomfortable at times. But if we face the music long enough it is certain to change. Do I take responsibility for myself or do I try to run away?

Higher Power, please grant me the courage to face my responsibilities today.

Higher Power, please help me cope with my pain today!

At one time, many of us were frantically seeking to kill our pain and in the process we almost killed ourselves. We would have gone to any lengths, even the ultimate act of suicide, to end our pain, but deep down our instinct was to live. All we wanted was relief.

But there were others who had for one reason or another, lost their instinct to live. For them, we need to pray that they have found their relief and that they and their families are now at peace with themselves. For those of us who are here today, we must learn from their actions. Not judge, but learn. Our lesson is that chronic pain has the ability and the strength to take away our instinct to live. Is my instinct to live today greater than it's alternative?

Higher Power, in the depths of my pain and despair, please show me how strong my instinct to live is.

Higher Power, please help me cope with my pain today!

Chronic pain is a community concern as well as a personal concern. It affects the young and old, people at our work place, our families, friends and the public at large. Who is responsible for helping with this problem? Surely there are many specialists, educators, doctors and the like who share the responsibility. We, however, share a responsibility to ourselves and to the community as a whole to do our part.

Whether we speak at a treatment center, lead a support group, further educate the community about chronic pain or reach out to others who are in pain, we will be sharing the responsibility. What once was solely a personal problem has become a part of our community. We may never rid ourselves or anyone else of pain, but together we can share our responsibilities and learn to cope with our pain one day at a time. Do I believe chronic pain is a community problem?

Higher Power, please help me realize I have a responsibility to myself and to my community when coping with chronic pain.

Higher Power, please help me cope with my pain today!

Many addicts have tricked themselves into taking one more pill or drink thinking it will relieve their pain or ease their emotional turmoil. They were wrong. It only made things worse.

Some have been fortunate to find their way back and others were not so fortunate. They are either down so deep they can't find their way back or they have moved on, never to return.

For we addicts, this is a life and death situation. We can't afford complacency or allow ourselves to get into the "stinkin-thinkin" that a pill or drink will help us. It won't! Do I believe a pill or drink will help relieve my pain and emotional turmoil?

Higher Power, please remind me that no amount of pills or alcohol will relieve my pain. It will only make things worse.

Higher Power, please help me cope with my pain today!

343

We have every right to be proud of ourselves for we have survived a profound trip to the depths of our despair and back. We have adjusted our lives accordingly and now live with our pain each day.

When others tell us we're not doing enough and we should do more, or that our despair wasn't that bad, we can politely say, "Thou shall not judge until you have walked a mile in my shoes." What do I say to others who don't understand my pain?

Higher Power, help me to have patience with those who don't understand my pain or where I have come from.

Higher Power, please help me cope with my pain today!

Some of us are so focused on getting back what we once had that we don't take time to reward ourselves for the work we have accomplished. Others may think rewarding themselves is sinful or they just feel too guilty to do it. Whatever our case, there's absolutely nothing wrong or sinful about rewarding ourselves. Whether it be for doing a good job at work, being a decent parent, or making it through a tough day, we deserve to reward ourselves. When we feel good about ourselves and what we've done, we can build from that and continue to move forward. But, by not rewarding ourselves, we are actually saying that what we're doing isn't good enough and probably never will be. Have I rewarded myself lately?

Higher Power, please help me take time out to reward myself today.

Higher Power, please help me cope with my pain today!

Chronic pain has caused many of us to say, "Lock-up, please." The pain has been so severe that some have wanted to take their lives just to stop it. Some of us just weren't sure where we could or should go. Our lives were turned upside down. We were full of fear and anxiety and overrun by pain. Most of all, we had feared what was happening to us.

We believe there is no need for embarrassment. Instead we deserve to pat ourselves on the back for seeking support. Remember, we are dealing with chronic pain and with chronic pain comes the need for support. So if and when our pain screams out, "Put me in lock-up," it is not an embarrassment to seek support, it's a necessity. Do I seek help when I feel my pain crying, "lock-up?"

Higher Power, please help me remember that help and support are available when I need it.

Higher Power, please help me cope with my pain today!

In the beginning, our pain slowly consumed us. Our love for ourselves and for others became covered by anger, fear, and resentment. We knew there was a time when we felt love for others and we certainly loved ourselves. But somehow our pain had over-shadowed that love. We wondered if we would be capable of love again.

As we learn to manage our pain, we find that what we were once angry at and what we once feared and resented begins to fade away. We come to realize that our love for ourselves and others has never left us. It was covered by our pain. Do I believe I am capable of loving myself and others today?

Higher Power, please show me that I am capable of loving myself and others today.

Higher Power, please help me cope with my pain today!

347

We are the survivors; the ones who have come from our own despair to start a new life. We are the ones with chronic pain. We are the ones who have feelings, families and loved ones. We are the ones who have come to love ourselves as we are. We are the ones who have goals and ambitions. We are the ones who have many talents and much to offer society. We are the ones who have dreams and the ones who dare follow them. We are the one with chronic pain. Do I believe in who I am today?

Higher Power, please help me accept who I have become today. Please help me accept I am the one who has chronic pain.

Higher Power, please help me cope with my pain today!

There is a time between climbing out of our despair and finding our direction that we may feel nothing but emptiness. An overwhelming sensation of loneliness and lack of expression is often present, only to be questioned and feared. Our lack of direction has shattered our hope and desire for the future. All that is left is our pain and a feeling of emptiness.

As our direction becomes clearer, our emptiness is replaced by hope and the desire to move forward. Our once lifeless face now has many expressions. Our loneliness has been replaced by friends we thought had once left us. Our once pitted stomach has been filled with a spirituality we thought was gone forever. Our pain however, still remains, but we no longer feel the emptiness we once did. Do I feel empty inside?

Higher Power, I know with you, I will never be empty inside. I know with patience and prayer, you will show me my direction.

Higher Power, please help me cope with my pain today!

At times we go about finding happiness like a bird perched in a tree waiting for it's next meal. We wait, hoping happiness will come our way. As a result, many of us are starving for happiness.

Today is a new day filled with lessons to be learned and happiness to be experienced. But when we sit perched on our branch, we are sure to miss a great share of it. We must remember, happiness comes from within. It is based on how we feel about ourselves and in turn, how we view the world around us. Happiness is not a by-product of life, rather it is something we can experience each day providing we are willing to search for it. Do I search out happiness today or am I waiting for happiness to find me?

Higher Power, please help me find the happiness that lies within me today.

Higher Power, please help me cope with my pain today!

Having chronic pain can seem like being on a roller coaster, at least in the beginning. One day we're able to go for a walk, work a full day or even exercise, and the next day we're paralyzed. We can go along like this for months wondering what is happening to us. We soon find we are on a roller coaster with our pain, wondering when the ride will be through.

When our pain no longer controls us and we begin to manage it, our ride will come to an end. We will discover there can be a balance in managing our pain. We will come to know our limitations and our strengths and weaknesses. We will discover we have more control over managing our pain than we had once thought. Do I continue to have roller coaster days or have I found a balance with managing my pain?

Higher Power, please give me the courage and strength to make it through my uncertain days. Please help me find a balance when managing my pain.

Higher Power, please help me cope with my pain today!

351

In the beginning our pain has stolen more moments from us than many care to admit. Moments with our spouses, our friends, our children, and many others. These are our stolen moments we cannot bring back.

Today, our insurance for reducing the number of stolen moments our pain may want to steal from us, is to work the best possible recovery we can. We will never retrieve the moments we have lost, but by managing our pain and not letting it manage us, we'll surely save more moments than we will lose. Do I allow my pain to steal moments from me today?

Higher Power, please help me accept that my stolen moments are in the past, but by managing my pain today, I will have many more moments to cherish.

Higher Power, please help me cope with my pain today!

Many of us at one time or another have been on our knees in pain; feeling hopeless. We were desperately looking for a trace of something that would bring us to our feet again. That trace of something was hope.

As time passed, our hopelessness was transformed into hope. We had discovered we wanted to fight more than we wanted to give up. Our hopelessness had become our greatest asset. Our lives had to improve. We couldn't see ourselves living in despair any longer. We wanted and believed our lives could change if we began feeling hope rather than hopelessness. Do I feel hope in my life today or do I feel hopelessness?

Higher Power, please help me see how my hopelessness has brought hope into my life today.

Higher Power, please help me cope with my pain today!

353

Pain is inevitable. Suffering is optional. That says it all for those of us with chronic pain. We have been told our pain cannot be avoided nor can it be prevented. It is inevitable. We have to learn how to live with it. No one had said that suffering was optional. Nor did they mention we can be reasonably content managing our pain. All we had known is our pain was inevitable. Do I know that my odds of suffering decrease when I manage my pain today?

Higher Power, please help me see that my suffering is optional. Help me realize that what pain I do have today is manageable.

Higher Power, please help me cope with my pain today!

Many of us have tools to cope with our pain and a great amount of determination or we would not have made it this far. By continuing to practice and put what we have learned into action, we are sure to lessen our chances of relapse or stumbling so far back that we cannot return.

Some continue to procrastinate and think this can never happen to them. Wrong. We are all at risk. When we take action we are taking out an insurance policy on ourselves. The worse may not happen, but we will be prepared anyway. Without taking action and practicing what we have learned, we are putting ourselves at risk. Have I learned to take action or am I one who procrastinates?

Higher Power, please give me the courage and patience to practice what I know today. Help me take action and not procrastinate.

Higher Power, please help me cope with my pain today!

355

Many of us go through the first weeks and months of managing our pain diverted from life's problems. We have found a renewed reason to live. Life was good. Then one day the honeymoon was over, the walls came crashing in, and we wondered what happened.

We had found that the world was ready for us, but we weren't entirely ready for it. Our old ways had surfaced and we were beside ourselves. In an instant, we had found there was much work yet to be done. We must not get too discouraged. There is hope. We must go back to what we have learned and begin putting it into practice. We must shift our attitude to one of, "I can" rather than one of, "I can't" and before long we will find ourselves back on track. Is the honeymoon over for me?

Higher Power, If I should slip backwards today, please help me regain my composure and set me back on my path of recovery.

Higher Power, please help me cope with my pain today!

In the beginning we spent a great deal of time hiding from ourselves and others. Many of us spent our time locked in our rooms or under the covers. If we could have found a cave we would have settled there. We went to great lengths to be alone.

As time passed, we realize running from our pain and ourselves was no longer effective. Our pain and problems had followed us everywhere we went. Wherever we had surfaced our problems had surfaced.

Our temptation today may be to regress back to being a loner. Thinking we can hide from ourselves and others. However our past experiences have proven otherwise. Once a loner, always a loner is not our case today. We can face our pain and whatever problem arises with patience and guidance from our Higher Power. Have I realized that I no longer have to hide from my pain and my problems?

Higher Power, help me realize that I no longer have to be a loner. With your help I can face whatever pain and problems I may have today.

Higher Power, please help me cope with my pain today!

Most of us at one time or another gave up being a citizen. Our pain had taken control of our lives. We assumed we were no longer the useful, productive citizens we once were. We began declining invitations to gatherings and relinquished our positions within our communities. This was the end for us. We were no longer a part of our community. Our pain had won, at least temporarily.

As we begin managing our pain our self-confidence and the desire to regain our status as a citizen grows. Some of us may return to our previous activities while others may search out new ones. Whatever our case, in time we have a chance to be a part of our communities and to be a citizen again. Do I believe I can become a part of my community again?

Higher Power, please give me the strength and guidance to become a part of my community today.

Higher Power, please help me cope with my pain today!

We were traveling down the road when suddenly
we had stopped in the middle of it. We were lost,
confused and frightened. Our pain worsened. The
sun fell below the horizon. We awoke only to find
ourselves exactly where we had stopped. Our pain
was too great to walk and no one was coming to help
us. We were alone in the middle of the road with our
pain.

Am I still alone in the middle of the road with my
pain?

Higher Power, please help me reach out to others for
help when I feel alone and frightened. Help me realize that there are others who can help me cope with
my pain today. I no longer need to be alone and
frightened.

Higher Power, please help me cope with my pain today!

For most of us, at one point or another our pain had become too much to cope with. We wanted out; we wanted relief. Taking our life had seemed like the only option left and we didn't care if we saw the morning. For many of us the morning did come and for others they would never see another.

For those of us who saw the morning, we were overcome by gratitude, followed by fear. We were still in pain and emotional turmoil, but we had another chance. We took to our knees. We had decided we wanted to go on living. We wanted to see the next morning. Do I want to see the morning come?

Higher Power, please take away my hopelessness and despair. Help me to see the next morning.

Higher Power, please help me cope with my pain today!

What do we do when we have extreme difficulties managing our pain or we're having a bout with depression or sliding into our old pain behavior? If we don't know, we need to find out. These are types of emergency situations for us that we need to cut off before they develop to their extremes.

One way to handle these emergencies is to be willing to tell someone how we're feeling and ask for the help we need. But some of us would rather have others think that we're doing great or we may worry that they will think less of us if we're not doing as well as they expect. So we don't ask for the help we need and our emergency situation escalates to it's extreme. Do I have a plan for my emergencies?

Higher Power, please give me the strength to reach out to others today. Help me learn how to avoid letting my emergencies get to their extremes.

Higher Power, please help me cope with my pain today!

Chronic pain has been associated with alcoholism, drug addiction, depression and suicide. If you have chronic pain and you are reading this, you're fortunate. You are one of the survivors. There are days when we may not feel so fortunate, but we are. Let us recall where we have come from and the progress we've made. This should remind us, we are truly one of the survivors. Do I feel fortunate that I am one of the survivors?

Higher Power, please help me realize I am one of the fortunate ones.

Higher Power, please help me cope with my pain today!

362

DECEMBER

Those of us who face our pain and our limitations each day are known as those who dare. We dare to face the known and the unknown, the believable and the unbelievable, the powerful and our power-lessness. We who dare face decisions of altering our lives and having our lives altered for us without warning. We are those who dare try a new beginning and dare to follow our passions and unfulfilled dreams. Today, we are truly those who dare. Am I one who dares?

Higher Power, please grant me the courage to become one who dares.

Higher Power, please help me cope with my pain today!

Today it is time that we come clean with ourselves, our families, and our friends. It is time we ask for support, not pity. We can only play on the emotions of pity for so long until it turns against us. Playing the pity game is dangerous for those of us with chronic pain. When we let ourselves, our families, and our friends express pity towards us, our recovery and all we have worked for is sure to slip away.

We know down deep that growth comes from support, not pity. Today we must begin confronting our feelings of self-pity and the feelings others project on us as well and begin asking for support. We may miss the attention that self-pity brings at first, but in time we will come to realize that the attention we receive from those who support us will more than make up for what we have given up. Do I ask for pity or support today?

Higher Power, please help me leave my self-pity behind and begin asking for support from my family and friends.

Higher Power, please help me cope with my pain today!

The day is cold and I am tired but there are many tasks that lie ahead. The days wind blows cold and my pain makes me tremble within it's captivity. This pain is all mine. I have tried to give it away and I have tried running from it, but it stays within me. What do I do today? Do I try running again or do I stay and fight my pain? Do I accept my pain and try to overcome it or do I have the same old conversation with it as I did yesterday and the day before that. I guess it's my pain, therefore I can do anything that I want with it, except get rid of it. How do I feel about my pain today?

Higher Power, please give me the courage to pause and face my pain today.

Higher Power, please help me cope with my pain today!

As the days go by our pain remains. Some days are more difficult than others but we have feelings of peace and serenity. Our opportunities have grown two-fold. Our fear of the future has faded. Hope is now plentiful. Our lives have taken directions many of us have only dreamed of. Our willingness to give of ourselves has become a priority. We no longer live in the past nor the future. For today, this is part of who we have become. If it is not, and we would like it to be, it can be ours if we ask for it. Am I thankful for who I have become?

Higher Power, today I thank you for who I have become.

Higher Power, please help me cope with my pain today!

Today, many of us have a new lease on life. We're alive. Some of us were close to death and others were well on their way. So how can anything we do for the rest of our days be anything short of a miracle?

Well, for some of us, everything is short of a miracle. We hardly seem grateful for what has happened to us. We have expressed little gratitude for the second chance we have been given. We've been offered new jobs, support, opportunities to learn how to manage our pain and more. Yet we think it's not like before. We think it's all second-rate stuff.

What we have today may not be as plentiful as before or as good as we think it should be, but it is a start. We must remember, all that has been given to us today is from our Higher Power and it is surely, first rate stuff. Am I grateful for what I have today?

Higher Power, please help me think of my things as gifts from you and not second-rate stuff.

Higher Power, please help me cope with my pain today!

Many of us have harbored resentments towards doctors, lawyers, employers and others. The doctors didn't take away our pain, the lawyers didn't do a good enough job, and our employers fired us. The others simply didn't understand what we were going through and expressed little concern.

Regardless if our resentments are from the past or they are new, they must be resolved. They cause stress, sleepless nights, pent up anger, and unnecessary pain. Our only chance is to clean house. Face our resentments and move on. Our resentments are like weeds. When not dealt with, they keep spreading throughout our body. Eventually we become ragefull, bitter people and we become consumed with pain. Today is our day to put the past behind us and move forward with peace and contentment. Have I dealt with my past resentments?

Higher Power, grant me the courage to face my past resentments and to begin moving forward.

Higher Power, please help me cope with my pain today!

You do not need to impress me, nor do you have to be special in any certain way to please me. Just love me and trust me. I don't require special prayer when spoken to. Talk to me as you would a friend and I will listen. If there are people you want to pray for, mention their names and I will do what is best for them. If you want a blessing for yourself in health or success, just ask. I will give you what is best. It may not be what you expected, but I assure you it will be best.

Share with me your self centeredness, your temper, and your pain. Do not be ashamed. I love you in spite of your shortcomings. Share with me your fears of today and tomorrow. Then trust yourself to trust in me, for I have blessings in store for you today. Do I listen to my Higher Power?

Higher Power, I understand that you love me and care for me in spite of my shortcomings. For that I am truly grateful.

Higher Power, please help me cope with my pain today!

For those of us with chronic pain, freedom may be what we want most. We no longer want to remain prisoners of our pain or the despair and depression it has left behind. We no longer want to wake up each day, only to be reminded that our lives have been taken away and replaced by emptiness and loneliness.

What we want is freedom. Freedom from all that has kept us prisoners of our pain and all that has stood in our way of recovery. But how do we get this freedom? We get it through acceptance and through our Higher Power. When we are freed, it will truly be a gift from our Higher Power. But it is also contingent upon our actions. We must do our part to be freed and to keep the freedom we so desperately want and need. Am I freed from my pain and despair today?

Higher Power, please show me what I must do to be granted freedom today.

Higher Power, please help me cope with my pain today!

Many of us have screamed out at our Higher Power in times of pain and confusion. All we were looking for was someone who would listen and understand. We didn't mean to place blame or to make threats at our Higher Power for all that has happened in our lives. But we did.

We must not get discouraged or lose all hope just yet. We may have tried to force our Higher Power out of our lives, but we really haven't. In spite of what we may have thought or said about our Higher Power, he or she has never left our side. It is we who have left in time of turmoil. Our Higher Power loves us unconditionally and at times in spite of ourselves. Do I know my Higher Power loves me unconditionally today?

Higher Power, I know that it is you who loves me and cares for me no matter what I may do today and in the future.

Higher Power, please help me cope with my pain today!

373

Many of us have grown to dislike or even hate our bodies. They may no longer do what we would like them to. They may be scarred or have taken on a shape that many of us have come to dislike or are embarrassed about.

Whatever our case, it is time for the healing to begin. It is time we make peace with our bodies. It is time to accept our bodies as they are today and to stop wishing we looked like we had in the past. It is time we come to accept our bodies new limitations and it's requests for gentleness.

It is time we grow to respect the one and only body we have, rather than hating it and trying to destroy it. Have I begun healing my body today?

Higher Power, please help me begin to let my body heal today. Please help me grow to accept myself as I am and not for what I was or think I could become.

Higher Power, please help me cope with my pain today!

We have found a gift. We have learned how to manage our pain. In the process we have gained peace of mind, wisdom, courage and ultimately, a new life. Many of us can remember at one time, we desperately wanted these things but they were nowhere to be found, until we found others who were like us.

Something magical happens when two people with chronic pain share with each other. We don't have to explain everything or make excuses. We have a common bond and a common goal. We want to cope with our pain and live our lives. Giving away what we have found will help us keep what we so desperately wanted and now have. Do I graciously give away what I have found?

Higher Power, please help me to realize that my new life depends on giving away what I have found.

Higher Power, please help me cope with my pain today!

When we're honest with ourselves we can remember just how crazy our lives had become. We can remember times when we were out of control. That our pain and our life's situations drove us to the edge of despair. It left us wondering if we would ever be the same again, and if so, how long would it take for this restoration.

Today this restoration can happen. We can have our sanity restored, have peace of mind, and have reasonable control over our pain and our lives. This will be partly our responsibility and part of our Higher Power's. Remember God helps those who help themselves. We are to put forth the effort to cope with our pain and deal with our life's situations to the best of our ability and then leave the results to our Higher Power. This will be a process of hope and one of patience and faith. But with time it can materialize. Do I feel my sanity returning?

Higher Power, please help me realize I can be restored to sanity. Help me have the patience and faith in our ability to make this materialize one day at a time.

Higher Power, please help me cope with my pain today!

Many of us who have chronic pain also experience some type of depression. For some it is mild and for others it is severe. Some use drugs and alcohol to cope with their depression and others hope it will just go away. Whatever our case, it is time for us to take our lives back and gain some sort of manageability over our depression.

We need to remember that we are not bad or unusual people. We have chronic pain and with pain there is depression. Coping with our depression will need to be done one day at a time and it may require special services of others. But remember, many before us have gone on to live happy and content lives just as we can. How do I cope with my depression today?

Higher Power, please help me realize that drugs and alcohol will not help lift my depression. It will only make it worse. Please help me seek out those special services when I need them.

Higher Power, please help me cope with my pain today!

Upon awakening each day we ask our Higher Power to help us cope with our pain and to guide us through the day. We ask that Thy will be done and to guide us to others who need our help. We ask for the courage and wisdom to face each situation that is put in our path.

We walk forward with faith and courage knowing our Higher Power will be beside us for the twenty-four hours ahead. We do our best to accept yesterday and not project into tomorrow. We ask that our Higher Power grant us the twenty-four hours that lie ahead. Do I live twenty-four hours at a time?

Higher Power, please be with me and guide me through this twenty-four hours.

Higher Power, please help me cope with my pain today!

The holidays can be a special time for many, and difficult for others. Stress is at it's peak and our pain has said enough already. Expectations are running high and we wonder if we will ever experience relief. What we have learned about managing our pain we must not forget if we want to enjoy ourselves over the holidays.

Our first reminder is to slow down and pace ourselves. We will get there whenever we get there. Our second reminder is we must relax. Taking time for ourselves and for prayer will help us remain calm. Our third reminder is to keep up our exercise routine. Finally we need to keep up our good spirits and have fun. Am I ready for the holidays?

Higher Power, please help me prepare myself for the holiday season one day at a time.

Higher Power, please help me cope with my pain today!

When we begin thinking we are unique and we no longer need to practice what we have learned, we have begun slipping backwards. Some of us think we may have a harder path to follow or that we may have more pain than others do. This may be true. But what we are truly sure of is, a slip is a slip. No matter who we are we can all slip backwards. We can slip right back to the beginning where our pain and despair had almost taken our lives. Today, having chronic pain and allowing ourselves to slip backwards is serious business. Do I think I am unique and immune from slipping backwards?

Higher Power, grant me the courage and strength to put what I have learned into practice so I may avoid slipping backwards.

Higher Power, please help me cope with my pain today!

The foundation of our new lives are being formed each and every moment of the day. Our Higher Power has a plan for each and every one of us. Some have impatiently waited for their plans to be revealed and others have come to the conclusion that all things will be revealed when the time is right and not before.

If we are impatient for our answers today, what will be asked of us will be most difficult to abide by, but it can be done. We must stay away from asking what our Higher Power's plan is for us today and begin to ask our Higher Power for the courage and strength to be a part in building our foundations. Layer by layer our foundations will become strong enough for us to stand on and then and only then can the divine plan from our Higher Power be revealed to us. Have I begun building my foundation today or am I impatiently awaiting all my answers?

Higher Power, please show me how I can help you build my foundation. Help me accept that when I am ready, you will reveal the answers I have been waiting for.

Higher Power, please help me cope with my pain today!

At one time or another, those of us with chronic pain have fallen down the ladder of life. We have lost many material possessions, our sanity, our self-respect, our spirituality, and ultimately ourselves. Our pain had taken us so far down the ladder that it has left us emotionally, physically and spiritually bankrupt.

In our recovery, climbing back up the ladder of life can only be done one step at a time. Many of us will become impatient and feel we should have reached the top of the ladder yesterday or even the day before that. But deep down, we know it doesn't happen this way. Climbing the ladder is a process and it will take time. If we are to rebuild our lives it will take patience, determination, and persistence. Am I willing to take whatever steps are necessary to climb the ladder of life?

Higher Power, please grant me the courage to continue my climb towards emotional, physical and spiritual growth one step at a time.

Higher Power, please help me cope with my pain today!

When someone has said to us, that what we have today is a gift from our Higher Power, many of us do not know how to respond. Some of us may have said to ourselves, not from the Higher Power I know. The Higher Power I know has been keeping score of all I've ever done and I'm losing. If this was true many of us would most likely not be in the position we're in today.

No matter who we are or what we may have done to ourselves or others, our Higher Power loves us and has many gifts to give, providing we are willing to accept them. As we grow to accept ourselves and our relationship with our Higher Power in our recovery, we will realize there is no one keeping score but ourselves. There is no one more capable of accepting or declining the gifts our Higher Power has for us but ourselves. Do I accept the gifts my Higher Power has for me?

Higher Power, please help me humbly accept your gifts today.

Higher Power, please help me cope with my pain today!

If you have had the satisfaction of hearing that laugh at the other end of the phone or seeing a friend's eyes light up with a warm smile when they see you, you most likely know what it's like to reach out and share yourself. Those of us with chronic pain also know that laugh and smile. We have a common bond. Pain and understanding. We know about each other, we understand each other and we care for one another.

Working with others who have chronic pain must become a priority in our lives. Whether we pick up the phone or meet for lunch, we are reaching out to others and sharing our common bond. From this we will see how our experience can help others and how they in turn can help us. Do I take to the phone or meet others when they need help?

Higher Power, please help me reach out to others, whether I am in need or they are.

Higher Power, please help me cope with my pain today!

Our Higher Power can grant us a daily reprieve from the elements of our pain. But this is contingent on our willingness to grow and our determination to manage our pain. But most of all, it is based on our spiritual condition.

We can be granted a daily reprieve from the insanity and the unmanageability of our pain and life's situations. As well as the uncertainty and the fear of our futures. This is not to say our pain will be completely taken away or that our lives will be perfect. It means temporary relief one day at a time. But when we put our program second and refuse to do what is asked of us, our daily reprieve will slip away. Do I know what I need to do for my daily reprieve?

Higher Power, please help me strive to do what is asked of me today for my daily reprieve.

Higher Power, please help me cope with my pain today!

But for the grace of God go I. How true this is for those of us with chronic pain. There are others who are less fortunate than we are. Yet in our daily lives we make our situations out to be worse than anyone else's. Sometimes we do this unconsciously and other times on purpose. Whatever our case, we cannot afford to forget about, for the grace of God go I.

What many of us have today we didn't have at one time. We have found new ways of managing our pain, we have felt peace, we have found fellowship, and we have been granted a second chance. A new life. These gifts and many more were given to us through the grace of God. They are for us to cherish and to share with others. For what we have today is truly by the grace of God. Do I feel grateful for the gifts that have been given to me today?

Higher Power, I know there are days when I complain and I seem ungrateful for what I have, but I truly believe I am blessed and I thank you.

Higher Power, please help me cope with my pain today!

The holidays can be a wonderful and joyous time. Hope and love is high on our list of gifts that we have received. But we must not forget our gratitude. We must not forget about the holidays that we have spent as prisoners of our pain. We must not forget the depression and the isolation. We must not forget that for some of us, it is a blessing to be alive and to be present for these holidays.

In the past, our pain controlled us to the point where all we had wanted was relief. Nothing else mattered. This year it can be different. We have the greatest gift of all to give to our families and friends. The gift of ourselves and gratitude. Am I grateful today?

Higher Power, I am truly grateful that I am able to share myself with others during the holidays. I truly realize that this is the greatest gift I can give.

Higher Power, please help me cope with my pain today!

Today we are truly children of our Higher Power. We are children of courage. We have been given true spirit. We have been face to face with our own death and insanity. Yet our courage and determination has emerged us to victory. But not before we had met the darkness of our souls and become prisoners of our pain. We had faced and resisted adversity to emerge wiser and stronger. This was not the path many of us would have chosen, but because of it we have truly become children of courage. Have I come to believe that I am a child of my Higher Power and that I have been given the courage to face each day?

Higher Power, I am grateful you have chosen me and for teaching me the true meaning of courage.

Higher Power, please help me cope with my pain today!

Today is a day we share with our family and friends. We give and we accept. We laugh and we cry. We are filled with hope and gratitude. We pray for and remember those who are no longer with us.

We take a moment to reflect back to where we were a year ago or years past. We realize how far our recovery has progressed and what we have left behind. We catch a sudden glimpse of where our journey may be taking us. We realize we have given of ourselves countless times in the past, just as asked. But today, it is time for us to accept the gifts that are presented to us. The gifts of peace, serenity, hope, freedom, of family and friends and of our Higher Power. We have given of ourselves and now it is time to receive. Will I accept the gifts that will be given to me today?

Higher Power, I am grateful from the bottom of my heart for the gifts you have given me and I accept them with the purest of intentions.

Higher Power, please help me cope with my pain today!

Today is a day filled with love for ourselves and others. It is a day to feel and express our gratitude, for we are alive. It is a day to remember those who have given their lives for relief from their pain and their emotional anguish. It is a day to recognize the thousands and thousands who will wake up today and live their life with pain.

It is a day for those of us who may feel alone and frightened. It is a day to extend our hand to others and share our experiences, strengths and hope. Finally, this is a day for all those around the country who have devoted their lives and their souls to working with those who have chronic pain. To you all I say, may your journey be safe and may your hearts be filled with love, peace and serenity. Dr. Z. am I doing my part to help others with chronic pain today?

Higher Power, please help me have the willingness to do whatever work you put in my path today. Help me realize that if it were not for others willingness to help, my recovery may not be what it is today.

Higher Power, please help me cope with my pain today!

Many of us with chronic pain have at one time or another asked ourselves, "Is this really happening. Is my pain real, or will it go away? Will I really have limitations or are they just kidding? Will my life really change that much? No, this can't possibly be real, or can it?"

A life with chronic pain is as real as it gets. We will be assured the opportunity of coming to terms with ourselves as never before. We will come to know our limitations and for some, our lives are sure to change. As for our pain, it is real and if it is chronic in nature, chances are it will not go away. But rest assured, it is manageable. Do I know a life with chronic pain is real?

Higher Power, please help me accept that my pain is real today. Help me realize that today I have the choice to cope with it or deny I have it.

Higher Power, please help me cope with my pain today!

391

One day many of us knew who we were and the next, well we really weren't sure. We had wondered just what happened. We wondered where our once comfortable lives had gone. We wondered why people were treating us as strangers when they once seemed to be our friend. We wondered why we had lost our job and why we had become depressed. We knew deep down we weren't the same person as we once were. We asked, "Where have I gone?"

Those of us with chronic pain have at one time or another lost ourselves. We had been thrust into a situation that was driven by pain, confusion, and plenty of uncertainty. But today, if all we have lost is ourselves, we can be grateful. Many others have lost their lives in this situation. We who remain, through the blessings of our Higher Power, have an opportunity to begin our journey to look for the lost self. Have I begun looking for what I may have lost?

Higher Power, please help me realize there is no need to look any further for what I have lost. All that I have lost lies within.

Higher Power, please help me cope with my pain today!

We all had our own set of tapes or messages that we told ourselves before our injury. Immediately following our injuries we began making new tapes. These new tapes or messages would be our profile and personality for some time to come. This information would be gathered from our family and friends, from the community, from doctors and others, and of course, ourselves.

They are our tapes. We have carefully put them together piece by piece. They have become a reflection of who we have become and how we feel about ourselves today. If we have discovered that we are uncomfortable with ourselves and the new tapes we have made, then it is time we change. Remember, we had the power to put these messages and tapes together, we certainly have the power to change them. What do my new tapes tell me today?

Higher Power, please help me begin replacing my negative messages with positive ones.

Higher Power, please help me cope with my pain today!

As our lives begin falling into place and we begin managing our pain with a degree of success, we can begin thinking that we'll never slip backwards again. We must be careful. Never is a long time. But more importantly, chronic pain has it's own way of doing what it wants and doing it when it wants to.

The way we cope with chronic pain is one day at a time. We prepare for our slips and flare-ups as if we expect them each day. We cannot deny or say never to the inevitable and expect to be fully prepared to rebound when our time comes. Today, it is time to refocus an attitude and outlook from never to when. Am I preparing myself for flare-ups and set-backs or am I living as if they will never happen to me?

Higher Power, please teach me how to prepare myself for the inevitable and not the never.

Higher Power, please help me cope with my pain today!

This year has not been perfect. But neither was last year or the year before that. For many of us it was a year of learning and relearning. A year with setbacks and triumphs. It was a year of discovery and one of acceptance. A year many of us moved one step closer to freedom and one step closer to our Higher Power. A year many of us learned that we cannot live in the past, but rather we can learn from it and move forward with hope, courage and wisdom. This past year has come and gone. It has brought many gifts and opportunities that we may not have had in years past. For today and for the year that has past, we can be thankful. Do I realize this past year was not perfect, but all that I was given was just what I need?

Higher Power, please help me understand that last year's successes and setbacks are for my learning and can be used for the year ahead.Higher Power, please help me cope with my pain today!

Higher Power, please help me cope with my pain today!

INDEX

398

400

ORDER FORM

Freedom Enterprises in Chronic Pain
P.O. Box 40220
St. Paul, MN 55104

Please send me _____ copy (copies) of Living with Chronic Pain One Day at a Time, by Mark Allen Zabawa. I am enclosing $8.95 (plus the appropriate sales tax) and $1.05 to cover postage and handling for the first book and $.50 for each additional book. Send check or money order—no cash or C.O.D.'s please. To order by phone, call 612-487-3611. Valid in U.S. only. All orders are subject to the availability of books.

Name _____

Address _____